WINGS ACROSS TIME

Flight Controllers

1. "On Remote". Wilf Sheffield,
TCA radio operator at
Oliver, B.C., circa 1939
2. Control Tower. Showing
radar screens and
controllers. Dorval present
day.

1

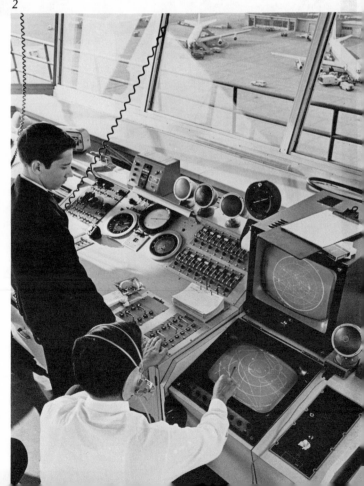

2

Refuelling Airplanes

3. *Lockheed Lodestar CF-TCV being serviced at Winnipeg in 1946.*

4. *DC-8 being refuelled from tanker truck.*

3

4

Cabin Service

5. Stewardess Annette Brunelle pours coffee from this enormous thermos for her passengers on the Lockheed 14, circa 1941.

6. Tristar coach comfort in the 19-foot-wide cabin of Lockheed's L-1011 TriStar, seats are in pairs, eight abreast. With two wide aisles running the length of the cabin, no passenger is more than one seat away from an aisle. (Photo courtesy Lockheed Aircraft Corporation).

5   6

Airports

7. Vancouver Airport, 1939.
8. Vancouver Airport in the 1970s (Photo courtesy Transport Canada).

7

8

Loading Mail and Freight

9. Mail being loaded aboard an early Lockheed Electra 1938.

10. Boeing 747 being loaded with freight. Note containerized cargo being lifted into the aircraft.

(Photo courtesy National Museum Science and Technology)

9

10

Ground Handling

11. Lockheed Super Electra being loaded with baggage, 1940.

12. Boeing 747 being prepared for take-off.

11

12

Simulators

13. *Boeing 747, built in Canada by CAE Ltd., Montreal.*

14. *Link trainer as developed by Edward Link. This wonder plane which never left the ground was invaluable in the training of pilots for TCA, 1940.*

13

14

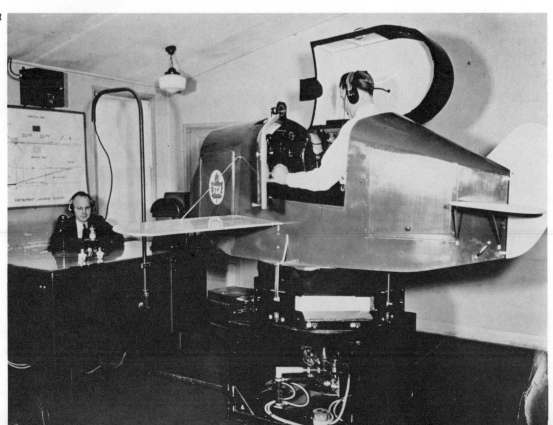

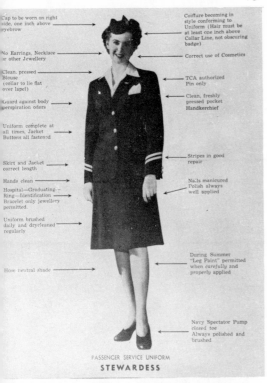

Cap to be worn on right side, one inch above eyebrow

No Earrings, Necklace or other Jewellery

Clean, pressed Blouse (collar to lie flat over lapel)

Guard against body perspiration odors

Uniform complete at all times, Jacket Buttons all fastened

Skirt and Jacket correct length

Hands clean

Hospital—Graduating—Ring—Identification Bracelet only jewellery permitted.

Uniform brushed daily and drycleaned regularly

Hose neutral shade

Coiffure becoming in style conforming to Uniform (Hair must be at least one inch above Collar Line, not obscuring badge)

Correct use of Cosmetics

TCA authorized Pin only

Clean, freshly pressed pocket Handkerchief

Stripes in good repair

Nails manicured Polish always well applied

During Summer "Leg Paint" permitted when *carefully* and *properly* applied

Navy Spectator Pump closed toe Always polished and brushed

PASSENGER SERVICE UNIFORM
STEWARDESS

16

Stewardess Uniforms

15. Third TCA uniform, worn 1941-1949. Navy blue in winter, grey in summer.

16. February 1970—Flare trousers in mix or match colours as optional wear, with sash belt, added to the mini-dress Air Canada uniform.

Stewardesses

17. Vancouver, 1938. Pat Eccleston and Lucile Garner, TCA's second and first stewardess respectively. They were the only ones to wear this beige uniform, which was very soon replaced by a navy blue.

18. Flight attendants' uniforms, 1977.

18

17

WINGS ACROSS TIME

The story of Air Canada

by DAVID H. COLLINS

GRIFFIN HOUSE

Toronto   1978

© David H. Collins, 1978
ISBN 0-88760-090-5

Published by Griffin Press Limited.
461 King Street West, Toronto, M5V 1K7, Canada

*(All the illustrations are from Air Canada unless otherwise
credited, and are reproduced here with their permission).*

Text design by Robert Garbutt

Printed and bound in Canada.

Canadian Cataloguing in Publication Data

Collins, David H., 1926-
Wings across time

Bibliography: p.
ISBN 0-88760-090-5

1. Air Canada — History. I. Title.

HE9815.A93C64   387.7'06'571   C77-001793-2

Contents

To the many people of
Trans-Canada Air Lines and Air Canada
both past and present,
who have made it possible
for us to fly safely
across Canada and the oceans beyond.

About the Author

David Collins was born in London, England in 1926. He was educated in the United Kingdom and is a teacher and a freelance writer, who teaches at Ryerson Polytechnical Institute in Toronto. David, a member of the Aviation/Space Writers' Association, has always had a passionate interest in both aviation and the sea. He is author of *Gold in the Cariboo* and *Wings of Progress,* both published by Clarke Irwin, Toronto, in the Canadian Jackdaw Series. David and his family live in Toronto, Canada.

THIS IS THE story of Air Canada and the thousands of people who have played a part in the operation of Canada's national airline. During the course of its forty-year history Air Canada has moved from the piston-driven age of the thirties to the jet-propelled superstar age of the seventies; from its three tiny aircraft mounting through the morning mists in 1937 to its fleet of jumbo jets criss-crossing continents and oceans nonstop in 1978.

It is impossible to mention more than very few people or events that have contributed to Air Canada's success. Much of the story is told in the many historic pictures accompanying the text. It is my hope that this book will serve as a tribute to the past and a glimpse of what the future may hold for Canada's national airline.

I WOULD LIKE to thank the following people for their help in making this book possible: Miss E. Buchanan, Manager, Historical Services, and Miss Betty Gabb-Jones, Air Canada, Montreal; Michael De Wilde and John Cavill, Air Canada, Public Affairs, Toronto; Michael Hildred, Air Canada, London, England; Hugh Whittington, Editor, *Canadian Aviation;* Mrs. Pat Maxwell, Captain Frank E. Smith, Captain and Mrs. G.B. Lothian, all formerly of Air Canada and TCA; David Russell, who did so much to guide this book along the right path; Drew Millar and Cecil Thom; Denis Barclay, and L.E. Sawyer and my wife Lorna and daughter Diana who lent me their support in this project.

I would like to thank the following companies and organizations for their assistance: Air Canada; Boeing Aircraft Company; McDonnell Douglas Aircraft Company; and Lockheed Aircraft Company Infoplan International, Toronto. Much of the research for this book was made possible by a grant from the Ontario Arts Council.

David H. Collins

I suppose we shall soon travel by air-vessels;
Make air instead of sea voyages;
And at length find our way to the moon,
In spite of the want of atmosphere.

LORD BYRON (1822)

THE EARLY EXPLORERS and the pioneers alike strove to open the gateways across Canada, many of them attempting their great treks from sea to sea. This dream finally became a reality when the steel of the railway forced its way across all natural barriers to bring the country together at the end of the nineteenth century. However, it was the invention of the incredible flying machine that finally brought the "global village" into being, and enabled Canadians to cross their own country within a few hours by air, rather than in days by land. Looking at the frail, fluttering flying machine, crossing the country by air seemed an impossible dream. Yet it was a vision of the future in which some men and women believed.

That vision became a reality in October 1920, when, using a variety of aircraft, the newly formed Canadian Air Force made the historic trans-Canada mail flight, from Halifax, Nova Scotia, to Vancouver, British Columbia. The entire distance of 3,265 miles was covered in 45 hours flying time, with numerous stops en route. The main reason behind the project was to gain vital experience for the airmen in long distance flying, and to investigate the possibility of establishing a network of air routes that would one day crisscross the entire country, and become part of a vast transcontinental air link.

The danger and adventure of flying in the First World War acted as a spur to the development of aviation. In the peacetime that followed many young men were imbued with a sense of challenge and expectation. Many of them had been too young to take part in the war, but were nevertheless thrilled by the idea of flying. It was these men who would eventually flock to Canada's growing numbers of flying schools to test their fledgling wings in the open skies. They swelled the ranks of existing pilots and ground crew personnel, who had learned their skills during the wartime years. These men were now faced with the very real prospect of earning a living in the not so *palmy* days of peace. It was their natural love of flying, and the knowledge they had acquired during the war of how to keep a plane airborne, that helped to make flying a part of modern life, and fostered the astounding development from the twenties to the present jet age.

Many of these pilots pioneered bush flying operations in Canada throughout the 1920s, particularly in the far North, where spluttering aircraft often landed alongside the more traditional dog teams. This band of flyers also opened the vital mail and freight routes that gradually formed the first aerial links between the various towns and cities across the country, thus carrying much-needed supplies into the more remote areas. Sometimes in these early days the planes also carried a number of wary passengers who were still a little dubious about the prospect of travelling by air.

During those first crucial days of civil aviation there was little to help the pilots in the way of modern navigational aids. Radios were often unreliable and radar had yet to be invented. Forced landings became a part of the everyday flying routine, caused either by bad weather or by faulty equipment. In fact, flying was only made possible by the pilot's skill and the infinite care given to the aircraft by the engineers and mechanics on the ground.

By the late 1920s and the mid-1930s aircraft were becoming more sophisticated machines, and a growing number of airlines had been formed in North America and other parts of the world. It was also during this period, hectic as it often was, that the public was thrilled by the exploits of the stars of the airways who proceeded to break the world's flying records. The achievements and high daring of these intrepid flyers were avidly read in the day's newspapers, and in certain cases their names became a legend in their own time. Many of those who became heroes or heroines simply disappeared over land or ocean. All of these pioneers left behind their knowledge from which today's network of air routes encircles the world.

Air transport has achieved the seemingly impossible in a very short period of history. The giant Boeing 747s that daily fly across Canada as part of Air Canada's fleet were made possible through the pioneering flight of J.A.D. McCurdy and his little "Silver Dart" biplane. On 23 February 1909 at Baddeck Bay, Nova Scotia, McCurdy became the first pilot in the British Empire to make a power-sustained flight. But the airline company that was to become the national carrier was not formed until the 1930s. The country was then in the midst of the great Depression; thousands of jobless people haunted the city streets in a fruitless search for work. Some men were lucky; they became part of a work force that helped create the vast trans-Canada airways system. This far-sighted work program to relieve unemployment was set up to improve airports and construct landing strips. A great deal of work was also done to develop navigational and radio aids in preparation for the time when air travel in Canada would be expanded.

The Department of Transport was formed at the height of the Depression, in 1936, with C.D. Howe as its first minister. From its inception this department took over the regulation of civil aviation in Canada from the Department of Defence. C.D. Howe became a firm voice behind the idea of forming a truly national airline designed to meet the needs of the Canadian public. It was also hoped that the new airline would become the last link in the chain formed by the existing British Commonwealth routes, that spread out from the United Kingdom to the Antipodes. But the plan was temporarily sabotaged when, in September 1939, the world was once again plunged into war.

Part One:

THE YEARS OF CHALLENGE   1937-1947

TCA airliner after its landing at Malton on a familiarization flight in 1938. This was in fact the first TCA aircraft to land at Malton Airport, Ontario.

None of us really foresaw what TCA would become. The reality has outrun our imaginations and an experiment has grown to a major achievement.

H. J. SYMINGTON,
President, Trans-Canada Air Lines, 1941-1947.

2

T*HE BILL SETTING* up Trans-Canada Air Lines was given royal assent on 10 April 1937. The moving force behind the establishment of TCA was C.D. Howe, and the company he had created would give the country a national airline.

The new company was to function as a wholly owned affiliate of Canadian National Railways, and would operate with a working capital of $5 million, consisting of 50,000 shares of common stock with a par value of $100 each. Its first president was C.N. President S.J. Hungerford (1937-41), who headed a team of able administrators from CNR.

Philip G. Johnson was appointed Vice President of Operations. An American, Johnson had been president of Boeing Aircraft Company and United Airlines, and was able to bring his valuable aeronautical knowledge to the new organization. His right-hand man was a Canadian, Donald MacLaren, a former First World War fighter ace, and one of the country's most experienced flyers, who had for a long time been a strong prophet for a national airline. He had been hired from Canadian Airways, which at the time was Canada's most versatile carrier. He quickly set up a TCA recruiting program for pilots that attracted a number of flyers, including J.L. Rood, H.W. Seagrim, George Lothian, W.W. Fowler, M.B. Barclay, Art Rankin, and R.M. Smith.

Trans-Canada Air Lines came into being at a time when travelling by air was still a rarity for the general public, who usually travelled across Canada by train. TCA in September 1937 possessed a fleet of just three aircraft—two Lockheed 10A's and a tiny Stearman biplane. These aircraft had been purchased from Canadian Airways, where they had been flown on the mail and passenger route between Vancouver, British Columbia, and Seattle, Washington, a route which was taken over at the time by TCA.

On 30 July 1937 the imagination of Canada was captured by the news that the Trans-Canada survey flight had taken place that day. The machine used on this occasion was a Lockheed Electra belonging to the Department of Transport. Its registration letters CF–CCT soon became known from coast to coast. The machine had been delayed by bad flying weather at St. Hubert, near Montreal, but finally was able to take off for Vancouver at 5:18 a.m. local time. The passengers were C.D. Howe, C.P. Edwards and H.J. Symington. The small Lockheed was captained by Squadron Leader J.H. Tudhope with Mr. John Hunter as his co-pilot. The machine also carried an engineer, Lou Parmenter, aboard for the long flight. The first leg of the 2,500 mile journey was to have been to Kapuskasing, Ontario, but owing to the weather the airplane had to refuel at Gillies, Ontario. By 2 p.m. the Lockheed had reached Winnipeg, the main hub of the

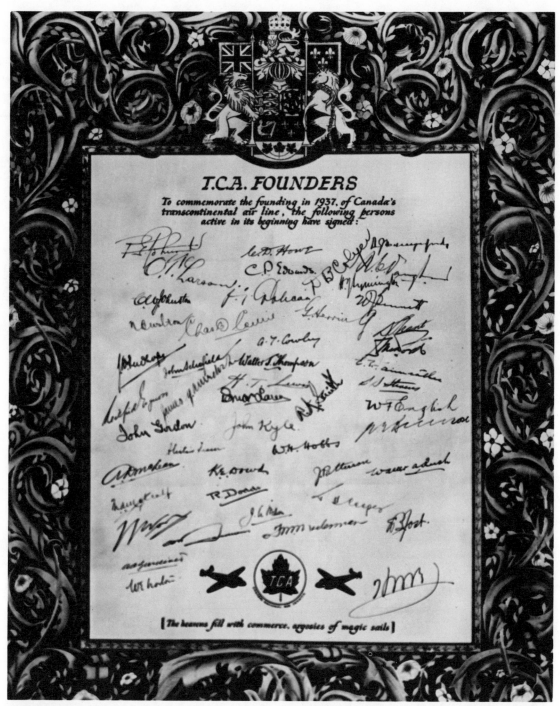

TCA founders

country's young air transport system. Further stops were made at Regina, Saskatche-wan, and Lethbridge, Alberta. The machine roared into the air from the tiny prairie airport for its long haul across the formidable barrier of the Rockies, which it had to cross before reaching the Pacific Coast.

At precisely 8:57 p.m. the exciting news was flashed out by airways officials in Vancouver, that the lone aircraft had reached Trail, British Columbia. At 6:29 p.m. PST the machine swooped down over Vancouver's Sea Island Airport for a perfect touch-down, with the gleaming discs of its two propellers coming slowly to a stop following a flight of 17 hours, 11 minutes. The survey flight over the projected TCA route had been completed successfully without any serious mishaps. A jubilant C.D. Howe left the aircraft to make an official statement to the waiting radio and newsreel commentators.

C.D. Howe speaks to the crowd in Vancouver

The Toronto *Globe and Mail's* headline for 31 July simply read "HOWE COMPLETES DAWN-DUSK FLIGHT."

The tasks facing TCA during its first months of operation were many. Air crews had to be trained, and new instrument and radio techniques had to be mastered, for the airline demanded high standards from all of its personnel.

The date of 1 September 1937 has a special place in TCA's history. On this day the company's first commercial flight from Vancouver to Boeing Field, Seattle, took place. The flight took off from Vancouver at 5 p.m. and covered the 122 miles to Seattle in 50 minutes. The aircraft's pilots were E.P.H. Wells and F.M. McGregor. During the months that followed a twice-daily service was carried on between the two cities every day except Sunday. The fare for the flight was $7.90 one way and $14.20 for the round trip. (Today the air fare for the same trip is $25 single or $50 return for the 35 minute jet flight by Pacific Western Airlines or United Airlines.)

The route was flown in 1937 in competition with United Airlines. In those early days flights were governed by strict regulations that required all flying to be done within certain fixed hours. No night flying was allowed into Vancouver Airport, which was not equipped for that purpose.

Mail was carried as well as passengers on these flights. The first TCA aircraft to fly to Seattle on 1 September, a ten-seater Lockheed Electra, had cost the company $55,234.55. The airline's total of fare-paying passengers for September 1937 was 144 persons. TCA ticket agents were provided with offices at Vancouver and Seattle where they were housed in the CNR ticket office. When the airline ticket agents went off duty, the tickets were sold by the railway staff.

That first flight in September was only the beginning. For the rest of 1937 TCA undertook daily training flights to familiarize the air crew with often complicated flight procedures, while at the same time completing necessary route structures. The radio and navigational links had also been expanded along the routes. During 1936 much of the groundwork had been done, including improvements to the airfields and the vital emergency landing strips across the country. Uncertain weather conditions often presented pilots with a real hazard, because the aircraft, including the Lockheed Electras, only had limited range. This made it imperative for them to reach their destinations before either bad weather or fading light overtook them en route.

By the 1930s great strides had already been made in aircraft design and radio equipment. In spite of these improvements aircraft were regarded by the general public with awe. The journey across the Rockies to the East was fraught with danger, including

NO. 1 AROUND THE WORLD WITH LOCKHEED

The Newest, Fastest Transcontinental Airline

Luxurious transports will speed these Montreal passengers to Vancouver in relaxing comfort. Perhaps few of them will be aware of the thrilling story of modern pioneering responsible for Trans-Canada Air Lines (T.C.A.), the newest and fastest transcontinental service.

Actually made-to-order, T.C.A. was created by Parliament in 1937. Arduous labor blazed the trail. Airports were hewn from virgin forests . . . endless survey flights made . . . up-to-the-minute ground and air equipment installed . . . personnel carefully trained. Today you can fly from Vancouver to Montreal, 2111 miles, in 14 flying hours—via one of the world's finest airlines.

As a passenger, you would see gorgeous northwest panoramas . . . enjoy the exhilarating power and freedom of air transportation . . . realize the great undertaking required to provide this modern, comfortable service . . . appreciate Trans-Canada's choice of Lockheed airplanes.

. . . and why Trans-Canada chooses Lockheeds

Performance with dependability was the chief concern —passenger comfort, cargo capacity, surplus power, long range were also important in selecting T.C.A. transports. The Lockheed engineering department collaborated with T.C.A. experts in providing every desired feature.

Accurate construction is just as important as careful engineering. Lockheed's large scale production utilizes modern precision machinery, assures accuracy. For example, in one eight-hour shift this giant hydro-press forms 5,000 metal parts with mathematical exactness.

Today's production line includes another group of Lockheed airplanes for Trans-Canada Airlines. 300 of a similar type are being delivered to Great Britain and Australia. These orders reflect the efficiency of the famous Lockheed Electras and the advance designing of the Lockheed 14.

THE SAME CHOICE HAS BEEN MADE BY 28 AIRLINES

Throughout the world Lockheed airplanes are providing fast, dependable transportation. Nome to Juneau, Bandoeng to Sydney, London to Warsaw, Algiers to Madagascar . . . over all six continents, in equatorial heat and through arctic cold. Everywhere an increasing number of travelers prefer airlines flying Lockheed transports. Wherever you go—whenever you can—fly Lockheed!

LOCKHEED AIRCRAFT CORPORATION
BURBANK, CALIFORNIA · REPRESENTATIVES THROUGHOUT THE WORLD

LOCKHEED

Look to
Lockheed for Leadership

Lockheed Aircraft Company advertisement that appeared in the press in 1939.

turbulent air currents that could hurl the little Lockheeds around the sky, as they made their way through the valleys before crossing the mountains. Today an Air Canada Lockheed Tristar can make the same flight by simply flying above the weather. The Lockheed Electras flown by TCA were among the most highly acclaimed aircraft in the world in 1937. For their time they were fast and ruggedly constructed; but their cabins were unpressurized, which meant that oxygen had to be used when crossing the mountains. The Electra's cruising speed at 5,000 feet was 185 mph, and it usually flew between 5,000 and 12,000 feet as it made its way through the valleys and over the mountains. An Air Canada Boeing 747 on the other hand can cruise at 570 mph at an altitude of between 30,000 and 35,000 feet.

By the end of 1937 TCA had further extended its training program to include flights between Lethbridge, Alberta, and Winnipeg, Manitoba. Stories reporting the airline's progress began appearing in magazines and newspapers. In spite of approaching war clouds and the fragile facade of the Munich Agreement, 1938, as far as TCA was concerned, was a period of steady growth. Throughout this busy year training flights continued, and night flying and instrument training were also speeded up. By midsummer of the same year the airline was running scheduled training flights as far as Montreal. A major maintenance base was set up in Winnipeg to serve the needs of TCA's expansion.

TCA hired its first stewardesses in 1938; until that time any inflight service required by passengers had been carried out by the aircraft's co-pilot. Stewardesses had been employed by airlines in the United States since 1930, when Miss Eileen Church was hired as an air hostess by United Airlines. The sight of a pretty girl waiting by the steps of a TCA airliner to welcome her small flock of passengers aboard often gave courage to the fainthearted. After all, if they saw an attractive girl in a smart uniform, who was obviously not afraid of flying, why should they be afraid themselves? In this respect, as in so many others, the girls were to prove themselves to be invaluable time and time again. Lucile Garner of Regina (now Mrs. J.A. Grant of Montreal) became the first stewardess to be accepted by TCA. Requirements for stewardesses were very strict: all were registered nurses and had to be under 5 feet 5 inches in height in their stocking feet (aircraft cabins were rather cramped in those days). Recruits also had to weigh under 125 pounds, had to be over 21 and in perfect health, had to have 20-20 vision, be unmarried—and above all, have their parents permission in writing! A great deal of the stewardess's training was carried out aboard the aircraft with literally an aircraft manual in hand, often travelling at the shattering speed of 180 mph. One reporter in 1938 suggested the prospective stewardess "must combine the comeliness of Venus with the capabilities of Florence Nightingale."

Today, an Air Canada flight attendant has to have a secondary school education and, when possible, be bilingual. She has to be physically fit and have a good personality. In spite of the larger aircraft now in service, the flight attendant's duties are still basically the same as they were in 1938.

During 1938 TCA established freight services on a regular basis between Winnipeg and Vancouver, and on 1 December of the same year similar services were extended as far as Montreal and Toronto. One of the main reasons for these flights was to further train aircrew for the latter routes. At the year's end TCA's staff had grown to a total of 332 employees, and its fleet consisted of fourteen Lockheed air liners.

However, the company's real goal of opening a passenger service across Canada still lay ahead. In spite of the approaching war TCA's staff were working at full speed toward the completion of the Trans-Canada passenger route during 1938 and early 1939. It was hoped that TCA's routes would finally extend to the east coast where the transcontinental route would join the British Empire & Commonwealth Air Link across the Atlantic to the United Kingdom. From Britain this huge web spread out to Asia and the Pacific where flight service was already in operation. But it was not until August 1939 that Imperial Airways (now British Airways) started an experimental airmail service across the Atlantic. Imperial Airways used the famous Short Empire flying boats for

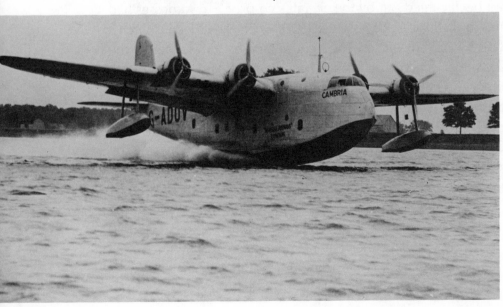

Short Empire Class flying boat of the type used by Imperial Airways on its Atlantic pioneer mail flights in 1939. (Photo courtesy British Airways).

The Mayor of Seattle and United Airlines stewardess greet TCA crew at the commencement of the company's first transcontinental flight on 1 April 1939. The fruit being presented was from U.S. cities on Pacific Coast for Mr. Hungerford in Montreal.

the flights. The route flown was Southampton (England), Foynes (Eire), Botwood (Newfoundland), Montreal, where servicing was carried out by TCA, and finally New York. The proposed service, together with the efforts being made by Pan American Airways was the first threat to the leisurely sea crossing, which at that time was still the domain of the magnificent ocean liners. Imperial Airway's experiments were brought to a halt with the outbreak of the Second World War.

TCA reached its first major goal on 1 April 1939, when, after months of preparation and training, the airline began its transcontinental passenger flights. During the same month the United States was getting ready to welcome its many international guests to the New York World's Fair, which was billed as the finest of them all. *Gone with the Wind* was being acclaimed with awards and praise. On 7 April the Toronto Maple Leafs played the Stanley Cup finals for the third time. However, for most of the world, the focus of attention was Europe.

The two Lockheed 14 H2's that inaugurated TCA's first transcontinental scheduled flights carrying fare-paying passengers took off simultaneously from Montreal and Vancouver. Advertisements had appeared in the newspapers for weeks prior to the flights:

The first revenue flight of TCA out of Montreal.

Mr. S.J. Hungerford in front of the Lockheed 14-H2 in which he flew from Seattle to Vancouver.

"TCA passenger service—leave Vancouver Island 6:45 p.m., lunch next day in Toronto or Montreal—daily commencing April 1st." The main claim made by the company on this occasion was not the number of passengers the machine carried, (which was only 10) plus the stewardess but the speed with which they spanned the country. Canada could now be crossed in fifteen hours by plane.

On the day of the first flight a cable was sent by S.J. Hungerford to all passengers on trip 1A from Montreal to Vancouver (the flight numbers resembled railway trip numbers in 1939):

> IT IS A GREAT PLEASURE FOR ME TO GREET YOU AS THE FIRST PASSENGERS
> OF THE TRANS-CANADA AIR LINES ON THE INAUGURATION OF REGULAR
> SERVICE BETWEEN MONTREAL, TORONTO AND VANCOUVER AND TO
> WISH YOU A FLIGHT YOU WILL LONG REMEMBER FOR ITS PLEASURE AS
> WELL AS ITS CONVENIENCE AND SPEED.

There is a legend that on those first two flights bottles of water taken from the Fraser and St. Lawrence rivers were broken over the nose of each aircraft, before they took off from Vancouver and Montreal.

The weather delayed the westbound flight for some thirty-four hours. Safety reasons had grounded the machine at Lethbridge, Alberta, as severe storms were raging in the area. The pilot, Captain Lewis Leigh, finally brought the Lockheed into Vancouver on 4 April. During this period he had attempted to cross the Rockies twice, and each time had been forced back to the Alberta side of the border. Captain Leigh told a *Vancouver Sun* reporter about his experiences. "It was snowing heavily when we left Winnipeg. We had fairly clear weather on the Prairies, but it closed up before we reached Lethbridge." In those days icing up was one of the main dangers faced by the aircraft. If the weight of the ice became too heavy on either the control surfaces or the engines themselves, control of the aircraft could be lost. As Captain Leigh said later in the same interview, "We struck the heaviest part of it when we reached the mountains. The plane started icing up heavily and I climbed to 17,000 feet, but it was icing all the way up, and we still could not top the clouds."

With the opening of TCA's transcontinental route the flying time between Montreal and the West coast was cut to between fourteen and fifteen hours, weather permitting. The route from Montreal and Vancouver was flown with stops at Ottawa, North Bay, Kapuskasing, Winnipeg, Regina, Lethbridge and Vancouver.

The cost of a ticket from Vancouver to Ottawa was $248.50 for the round trip in 1939. The rail fare for the same trip, including meals, berth and estimated tips was

Lockheed 14-H2 which inaugurated TCA's first revenue passenger flight from Vancouver to Winnipeg 1 April 1939.

| PACIFIC TIME | MOUNTAIN TIME | CENTRAL TIME |

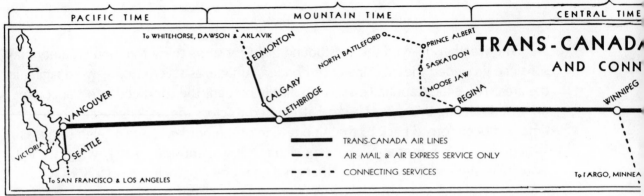

TRANS-CANADA
AND CONN...

TRANS-CANADA AIR LINES
—·—·— AIR MAIL & AIR EXPRESS SERVICE ONLY
- - - - - CONNECTING SERVICES

To WHITEHORSE, DAWSON & AKLAVIK
To SAN FRANCISCO & LOS ANGELES
To FARGO, MINNEA...

MONTREAL-WINNIPEG-VANCOUVER-VICTORIA
TRIP SCHEDULES — DAILY

Westbound—Read Down / Eastbound—Read Up

Trip No.	Trip No.	Trip No.	Miles	Table No. 1	Time	Trip No.	Trip No.	Trip No.
	1						2	
...	9.00 PM	...	0	Lv **Montreal**.....Ar	EST	...	12.15 PM	...
...	9.50 PM	...	110	Ar **Ottawa**......Lv	"	...	11.25 AM	...
...	10.00 PM	...		Lv **Ottawa**......Ar	"	...	11.15 AM	...
...	11.25 PM	...	307	Ar **North Bay**...Lv	"	...	9.50 AM	...
...	11.40 PM	...		Lv **North Bay**...Ar	"	...	9.35 AM	...
...	1.25 AM	...	575	Ar **Kapuskasing**.Lv	"	...	7.50 AM	...
...	1.35 AM	...		Lv **Kapuskasing**.Ar	"	...	7.40 AM	...
...	3.20 AM	*	870	Ar **Wagaming**...Ar	"	...	6.41 AM	...
...	4.55 AM	...	1242	Ar **Winnipeg**...Lv	CST	...	3.25 AM	...
...	5.10 AM	...		Lv **Winnipeg**...Ar	"	...	3.10 AM	...
...	6.25 AM	...	1575	Ar **Regina**......Lv	MST	...	12.20 AM	...
...	6.35 AM	...		Lv **Regina**......Ar	"	...	12.10 AM	...
...	8.55 AM	...	1942	Ar **Lethbridge**..Lv	"	...	10.05 PM	...
...	9.10 AM	...		Lv **Lethbridge**..Ar	"	...	9.50 PM	...
...	11.10 AM	...	2411	Ar **Vancouver**..Lv	PST	...	6.15 PM	...

9-A ex. Sun.	1-A Daily #	15-A ex. Sun.		Via Canadian Airways Ltd.		10-A ex. Sun.	16-A ex. Sun.	2-A Daily
9.00 AM	11.30 AM	3.00 PM	0	Lv **Vancouver**...Ar	PST	10.30 AM	2.00 PM	4.40 PM
9.30 AM	12.10 PM	3.30 PM	53	Ar **Victoria**......Lv	"	10.00 AM	1.30 PM	4.00 PM

TORONTO-WINNIPEG-VANCOUVER-VICTORIA
TRIP SCHEDULES — DAILY

Westbound—Read Down / Eastbound—Read Up

Trip No.	Trip No.	Trip No.	Miles	Table No. 2	Time	Trip No.	Trip No.	Trip No.
	21						22	
...	10.00 PM	...	0	Lv **Toronto**......Ar	EST	...	11.15 AM	...
...	11.20 PM	...	187	Ar **North Bay**....Lv	"	...	9.55 AM	...
	1						2	
...	11.40 PM	...		Lv **North Bay**....Ar	"	...	9.35 AM	...
...	1.25 AM	...	455	Ar **Kapuskasing**.Lv	"	...	7.50 AM	...
...	1.35 AM	...		Lv **Kapuskasing**.Ar	"	...	7.40 AM	...
...	3.20 AM	*	750	Ar **Wagaming**...Ar	"	...	6.41 AM	...
...	4.55 AM	...	1122	Ar **Winnipeg**...Lv	CST	...	3.25 AM	...
...	5.10 AM	...		Lv **Winnipeg**...Ar	"	...	3.10 AM	...
...	6.25 AM	...	1455	Ar **Regina**......Lv	MST	...	12.20 AM	...
...	6.35 AM	...		Lv **Regina**......Ar	"	...	12.10 AM	...
...	8.55 AM	...	1822	Ar **Lethbridge**..Lv	"	...	10.05 PM	...
...	9.10 AM	...		Lv **Lethbridge**..Ar	"	...	9.50 PM	...
...	11.10 AM	...	2291	Ar **Vancouver**..Lv	PST	...	6.15 PM	...

9-A ex. Sun.	1-A Daily #	15-A ex. Sun.		Via Canadian Airways Ltd.		10-A ex. Sun.	16-A ex. Sun.	2-A Daily
9.00 AM	11.30 AM	3.00 PM	0	Lv **Vancouver**...Ar	PST	10.30 AM	2.00 PM	4.40 PM
9.30 AM	12.10 PM	3.30 PM	53	Ar **Victoria**......Lv	"	10.00 AM	1.30 PM	4.00 PM

VANCOUVER - SEATTLE
TRIP SCHEDULES — DAILY

Southbound—Read Down / Northbound—Read Up

Trip No.	Trip No.	Trip No.	Miles	Table No. 3	Time	Trip No.	Trip No.	Trip No.
	6	4				3	5	
...	7.05 PM	11.45 AM	0	Lv **Vancouver**... Ar	PST	10.55 AM	5.40 PM	...
...	8.00 PM	12.40 PM	122	Ar **Seattle**...... Lv	"	10.00 AM	4.45 PM	...

EDMONTON - CALGARY - LETHBRIDGE
TRIP SCHEDULES — DAILY

Southbound—Read Down / Northbound—Read Up

Trip No.	Trip No.	Trip No.	Miles	Table No. 4	Time	Trip No.	Trip No.	Trip No.
	8	10				9	7	
...	6.40 AM	7.35 AM	0	Lv **Edmonton**... Ar	MST	12.25 AM	11.25 AM	...
...	7.50 AM	8.45 AM	175	Ar **Calgary**...... Lv	"	11.15 AM	10.15 AM	...
...	8.00 AM	8.55 AM		Lv **Calgary**...... Ar	"	11.05 AM	10.05 AM	...
...	8.50 AM	9.45 AM	288	Ar **Lethbridge**... Lv	"	10.15 AM	9.15 AM	...

MONCTON - MONTREAL - OTTAWA - TORONTO
TRIP SCHEDULES — DAILY

Westbound—Read Down / Eastbound—Read Up

Trip No.	Trip No.	Trip No.	Miles	Table No. 5	Time	Trip No.	Trip No.	Trip No.
23	22	11				12	21	24
Ⅹ3.00 PM	...	...	0	Lv **Moncton**....Ar	AST	...	...	Ⅹ 2.15 PM
Ⅹ4.45 PM	...	...	428	Ar **Montreal**...Lv	EST	...	...	Ⅹ11.00 AM
6.00 PM	...	8.30 AM		Lv **Montreal**...Ar	"	9.45 PM	...	10.45 AM
6.50 PM	...	9.20 AM	538	Ar **Ottawa**.....Lv	"	8.55 PM	...	9.55 AM
7.00 PM	...	9.30 AM		Lv **Ottawa**.....Ar	"	8.45 PM	...	9.45 AM
...	9.55 AM	...		Lv **North Bay**...Ar	"	...	11.20 PM	...
8.45 PM	11.15 AM	11.15 AM	764	Ar **Toronto**....Lv	"	7.00 PM	10.00 PM	8.00 AM

Direct connection is made for passengers from the Maritime
Provinces at St. Hubert Airport (Montreal), from Canadian
National Railways' "Ocean Limited" to Trip No. 11
for Ottawa and Toronto. The "Ocean Limited" will
stop at the Airport to discharge through passengers.

* Flag stop only.
\# Or after arrival of Trans-Canada Air Lines' Trip No. 1.
Ⅹ Air Mail and Air Express only between Moncton and
Montreal.

TRAVEL BY AIR—SEE MORE—DO MORE

AIR EXPRESS SAVES DAYS AND DOLLARS

TCA Schedule Nov. 1, 1939

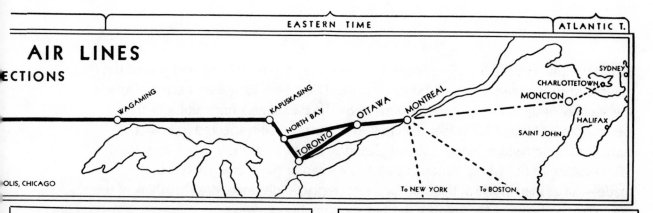

EASTERN TIME   ATLANTIC T.

AIR LINES
ECTIONS

WAGAMING   KAPUSKASING   NORTH BAY   OTTAWA   MONTREAL   MONCTON   SYDNEY   CHARLOTTETOWN   HALIFAX   SAINT JOHN   TORONTO

OLIS, CHICAGO   To NEW YORK   To BOSTON

CONDENSED SCHEDULES — Table No. 6
AIRLINE CONNECTIONS IN CANADA
TO AND FROM — VANCOUVER — EDMONTON — REGINA — WINNIPEG — MONTREAL

FOR TRANS-CANADA AIR LINES' SCHEDULES SEE TABLES 1, 2, 3, 4 and 5.

VANCOUVER—Connect with Canadian Airways, Yukon Southern Air Transport Ltd. and Ginger Coote Airways for:
Victoria and other Vancouver Island and B.C. Coast Ports of call, also Zeballos, Williams Lake, Quesnel, Prince George, Fort St. John, Whitehorse, Dawson, Germansen Landing-Fort St. James and Ware.

EDMONTON—Connect with Mackenzie Air Service, Canadian Airways and Yukon Southern Air Transport Ltd. for:
McMurray – Goldfields – Ft. Smith, Resolution – Yellowknife – Port Radium – Coppermine, Resolution – Simpson – Norman – Aklavik – Herschel Is. – Gordon Lake, Peace River – Vermillion, Fort St. John (Connect with Ginger-Coote Airways from Vancouver – Prince George) Ft. Nelson, Whitehorse (connect with White Pass & Yukon Route for Dawson, Fairbanks and Yukon).

REGINA—Connect with Prairie Airways for:
Moose Jaw, Saskatoon, Prince Albert and North Battleford. Connect at Prince Albert with Canadian Airways and M. & C. Aviation Co., for: Lac La Ronge, Ile a La Crosse- LaLoche, Fond du Lac – Goldfields – Ft. Smith (Connect with Canadian Airways, Mackenzie Air Service, Yukon Southern Air Transport.

WINNIPEG—Connect with Canadian Airways Ltd., Wings Limited and Starratt Airways and Transportation Ltd., for:
Berens River – Cross Lake – Island Lake – McKenzie Island – Gods Lake – Ilford – Sachigo River, Beresford Lake, Red Lake – Kenora – Goldpines – Hudson – Uchi Lake – Sioux Lookout – Central Patricia & Pickle Crow and other Central Manitoba and Northern Ontario mining centres.
Also connect at Winnipeg with Canadian National Railways for The Pas or Flin Flon, Man., connecting with Arrow Airways for: Cumberland House – Sturgeon Landing, Herb Lake, Sherridon, Cranberry Portage, Pelican Narrows and Island Falls.
Connect with Northwest Airlines for Fargo, St. Paul –Minneapolis and Chicago.

MONTREAL—Connect with Canadian Airways and Dominion Skyways for service to all Northern Quebec mining centres, also Quebec Airways weekly service to Rimouski in connection with incoming and outgoing ocean liners.
Connect with Canadian National Railways for Moncton thence Canadian Airways for Summerside, Charlottetown, Saint John and Halifax. (Service Saint John-Halifax direct via Maritime Airlines).
Connect with Canadian Colonial Airways for New York, also Central-Vermont Boston-Maine Airways for Burlington, Barre-Montpelier, Concord, Manchester and Boston.

Note:—Schedules and fares to various points mentioned on other Canadian airlines will be furnished at any Trans-Canada Air Lines office upon request.

AIR LINE CONNECTIONS IN THE UNITED STATES
TO AND FROM AIRPORTS AT CITIES LISTED

Table No. 7.   **Via Seattle, Wash.**

READ DOWN		Via Trans-Canada Air Lines to Seattle. Also service by United Air Lines.	READ UP	
7.05 PM	11.45 AM	Lv. VANCOUVER......(PST) TCA Ar.	10.55 AM	5.40 PM
8.00 PM	12.40 PM	Ar. SEATTLE.......... " " Lv.	10.00 AM	4.45 PM
8.50 PM	3.00 PM	Lv. SEATTLE..........(PST) UAL Ar.	7.52 AM	6.37 PM
9.55 PM	4.05 PM	Ar. PORTLAND....... " " Lv.	6.47 AM	5.30 PM
2.33 AM	8.35 PM	Ar. SAN FRANCISCO... " " Lv.	2.11 AM (Oakland)	....
5.34 AM	10.55 PM	Ar. LOS ANGELES (PST) UAL Lv.	11.05 PM	....

Via Winnipeg, Man.

From Vancouver	From Montreal	(For Complete Trans-Canada Air Lines' Schedules, See Tables 1, 2, 3, 4 & 5.)	For Montreal	For Vancouver
3.10 AM	4.55 AM	Ar. WINNIPEG........(CST) TCA Lv.	3.25 AM	5.10 AM
5.00 PM	5.15 AM	Lv. WINNIPEG........(CST) NWA Ar.	3.55 AM	9.55 AM
8.45 PM	9.00 AM	Lv. MINNEAPOLIS- (ST. PAUL)... " " Lv.	12.10 AM	6.15 AM
11.40 PM	11.25 AM	Ar. CHICAGO......... " " Lv.	9.30 AM	3.30 AM

Via Montreal, Que.

From Vancouver		(For Complete Trans-Canada Air Lines' Schedules, see Tables 1, 2, 3, 4 & 5.)	For Vancouver	
	12.15 PM	Ar. MONTREAL......(EST) TCA Lv	9.00 PM	
2.00 PM	7.00 PM	Lv. MONTREAL......(EST) CCA Ar	8.30 PM	5.10 PM
4.10 PM	9.30 PM	Ar. NEW YORK (Newark Airport) Lv. (EST) CCA	6.20 PM	3.00 PM
9.00 AM	2.45 PM	Lv. MONTREAL......(EST) BME Ar.	4.57 PM	11.52 AM
11.30 AM	5.15 PM	Ar. BOSTON......... " " Lv	2.30 PM	9.25 AM

AIR MAIL

Air Mail is fast and economical. In less than twenty-four hours, a letter can travel from East or West, the full span of the Dominion, for only 6¢ an ounce. Connecting air lines are available to fly it to any corner of Canada, or to many cities of the United States.

Air Mail letters do not have to be posted in a special letter box, but may be dropped in the same receptacle as ordinary letters. Simply mark your envelope "Via Air Mail" and affix ordinary postage stamps.

SEND YOUR LETTERS VIA AIR MAIL   ASK FOR AIR MAIL REPLY

14

$211.50. However, the travelling time for the one-way trip by rail required several days compared to fourteen or fifteen hours by plane. During the long flights across Canada the scenery of the country could be viewed by the passengers from altitudes that varied from 5,000 to 17,000 feet. Torchey Anderson, a well-respected journalist, summed up the flight in April's issue of *Canadian Aviation* in 1939, when he wrote: "The essence of the whole matter is that a new map of the Dominion has been made—an air map in which the time factor has replaced distance. We shall think of the west coast as being not so many miles but so many hours away."

Captain R.M. Smith, who commanded the Winnipeg–Toronto leg of TCA's first transcontinental flight reported these facts. "The crew, consisting of the First Officer, the stewardess and myself reported to the field at 3:00 a.m. We then received our normal weather briefing from the forecaster. After the briefing we made up our Flight Plan with the dispatcher. We taxied out at 4:10 a.m. in our twin-engined Lockheed, which carried our capacity load of ten passengers plus crew. The passengers included a baby ten months old. We received our clearance by radio from the dispatcher, because as yet there were no control towers in operation."

TCA enforced strict safety regulations and before any aircraft took off a Clearance Authorization Sheet had to be signed by the flight dispatcher. The pilot had to sign his

Winnipeg hangar, 1939. Two lockheed 14s and a Lockheed 10A being overhauled.

Blind flying check in TCA Lockheed 14, 1938.

Interior of Lockheed Super Electra, 1940.

name to the following statement: "I hereby acknowledge receipt of the foregoing clearance and accept the aircraft as being airworthy. Having analyzed and discussed weather reports, I now consider conditions suitable for the scheduled flight in accordance with existing regulations." After all, these were the days when the loss of a mailbag could result in a fine of $25 on each of the ground crew, and a qualified mechanic's wages were about $135 a month. In 1939 everyone worked hard and lent a hand when needed. Morale was very high in the new airline.

The stewardesses became the main form of communication between the captain and the passengers. These capable girls would answer questions from the passengers, and help them if they were in distress, or suffering from airsickness. The flights in 1939 were long and slow, as the aircraft always flew at the mercy of the weather. In 1939 the meals consisted of boxed lunches made up of either cold cuts or sandwiches plus fresh fruit.

With the outbreak of war in September 1939, TCA, along with the country's other transport services, went onto a wartime footing. During the first months of the conflict more and more of the airline's passengers appeared in uniform or were engaged in essential war services. Many men and women in TCA joined the armed forces, whilst the others kept a still expanding airline functioning.

TCA no longer shared the skies with bush and other working aircraft, for the airways were also used by military traffic at times. Security was tightened around the nation's airports, and TCA's personnel were asked to report any suspicious-looking people. In all the company's passenger and air express services priority was given to the armed forces. The needs of the war industries came next, and finally the nonessential services. Because of air transport, spare parts which might be vitally needed by a factory, could be flown into an area within hours rather than days.

During the first years of the war D.B. Colyer was appointed the company's Vice-President of Operations. At the same time improvements were made to TCA's maintenance bases at Montreal and Toronto, which were becoming important centres for the airline's growing operations. In spite of the airline's non-aggressive role, the need for its

Pilot Herb Hopson wearing his oxygen mask on a TCA flight in a Lockheed 14-H-2, 1940.

TCA aircraft over the Rockies. Note the aircraft's size compared to the mountains below, 1941.

services was steadily increasing in a manner that could never have been matched in the less hectic days of peace. Airline services provided the fastest means of transport in the country, and often military aircraft were not available for purely transport duties.

In spite of all the care given to TCA aircraft on the ground weather conditions still affected their schedules. This was a very real fact of life on the mountain section of the transcontinental route. Lethbridge, Alberta, became a staging post for flights in either

A night scene showing TCA aircraft on the ramp at Lethbridge, Alberta, April 1943. Note the flare path lights in the background.

direction. During bad spells an aircraft could be stranded there for anything from four hours to four days until the weather had cleared. Here again the reassuring attitude of the stewardess calmed many a passenger's anxiety or irritation over the delay. The Marquis Hotel at Lethbridge became the home base for many a grounded flight. The hardworking stewardess had the job of looking after the passengers on the ground as well as in the air, especially around departure time, to see that they hadn't strayed away on their own. To pass the long waiting hours bridge games were often organized as well as sessions around the hotel's piano.

Engine failure, as always with aircraft, was something that happened on occasion. One particular TCA flight was forced to make an emergency landing at Cranbrook, British Columbia, and after it had finally touched down dozens of local people came out to the airport to have a look at the machine. In those days people were very hospitable to both the aircrew and passengers alike. The local press gave the Cranbrook incident front page coverage, and the headline that appeared in the local paper the next day read: "GIANT TCA AIRCRAFT LANDS AT CRANBROOK."

By 31 December 1939 TCA was flying 9,044 miles on a daily scheduled basis. The crowded skies were shared by commercial aircraft and also by a steadily growing number of Royal Canadian Air Force machines. However, TCA employees could only join the services with the company's permission, for in many cases their jobs were essential. In spite of the war, plans were made by TCA to increase the route structure, including possible flights to New York and Buffalo. In 1940 Trans-Canada Air Lines became fully committed to the struggle to meet the demands of a country at war. The company took on active war work and the Winnipeg maintenance shops were en-

Some of TCA's Lockheed Aircraft lined up, 1940.

larged to provide necessary spare parts for RCAF aircraft, for everything that could possibly fly had to be carefully maintained.

Throughout 1941 the airline maintained its load of war work, and also took on the job of maintaining and overhauling BOAC's (now British Airways) aircraft. These machines had been flying with the vital Atlantic Return Ferry Service, which brought ferry pilots, who had flown much needed warplanes to Britain, back to Canada to pick up other machines. Invaluable work was done by these wartime ferry crews on Atlantic flying. Much of today's knowledge concerning transatlantic flying is based upon their operations. Bases were established at Gander in Newfoundland, and also in Greenland and Iceland. The ferry crews were a varied group, ranging from experienced transatlantic airline pilots to young fresh-faced airforce officers together with a large number of civilians. Their services were needed by the war effort because new aircraft had to be delivered to Britain as quickly as possible.

In spite of the war TCA extended its services during 1941 to include flights from Toronto to New York. During the same year Mr. H.J. Symington was appointed President of TCA—a post he held until 1947. The larger and more powerful Lockheed Lodestars became part of TCA's fleet and commenced invaluable work. At the year's end the company's personnel had grown to 1,123 persons, including 155 women, who in many cases were working alongside the men doing war work. The Winnipeg instrument shop was enlarged to overhaul RCAF instruments. By now Canada was on a firm war footing, and every available man and woman was doing something either in the armed forces or in industry.

Stewardess training, 1940. Note the stewardess in the Link trainer.

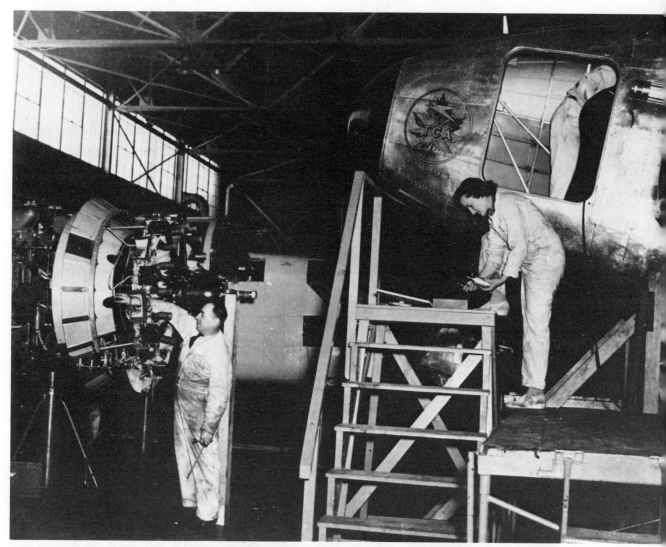

TCA base Winnipeg, 1943-44 showing men and women overhauling TCA and RCAF aircraft.

On 20 July 1941 a letter was sent to Mr. D.B. Colyer at TCA from the Minister of Munitions and Supply in Ottawa:

Mr. Hungerford has indicated to me that you and the operating staff of Trans-Canada Air Lines are somewhat restive in that you feel that you are not taking a full part in Canada's war effort. I feel that this situation arises out of a mistaken view of the situation as a whole. I am satisfied that Canada's munitions programme would be greatly hampered by any curtailment of air transportation, and I know that the Service Departments share this opinion as affecting the efficiency of their work . . .

The airplanes of Trans-Canada not only form a necessary part of Canada's wartime transportation, but also constitute a reserve of troop carriers immediately available when needed.

At the time this letter was written the workshops of TCA were working three shifts a day, and its fleet was carrying an increasing number of people on war work during that frantically busy year.

On 1 May 1942, St. John's, Newfoundland, was added to TCA's destinations. This new route provided a daily round trip between St. John's and Moncton, New Brunswick, and turned a trip that took days by surface transport into a flight of just five hours. Newfoundland, strategically placed as it was to meet the needs of war, was now

TCA Lockheed Lodestar after a belly landing at Gander, Newfoundland, early 1940s.

linked by passenger and air express service to the more important centres on the mainland. These important steps now joined the country together from coast to coast by air. In this way TCA provided much needed additional wartime services. Also in 1942 Canadian Pacific Airlines was formed, when the CPR purchased a number of financially pressed bush carriers and brought them together as a new airline. Canada now had two large airlines, and very quickly a spirit of active competition grew up between them that has persisted to the present. However, in 1942 TCA was facing a new challenge that led the company directly to the beginnings of its transatlantic operations.

In early 1943 TCA crews took on the operation of the Canadian Government Transatlantic Air Service. The basic concept for this operation came from C.D. Howe's highly active mind, as he said in June 1943: "During the past year they [the Canadian Armed

G.B. Kerr, steward, purser in the tiny galley of a TCA Lancastrian on transatlantic service, 1945.

Pilot Herb Hopson and Stewardess Betty Walsh boarding a TCA aircraft at Malton Airport, 1943.

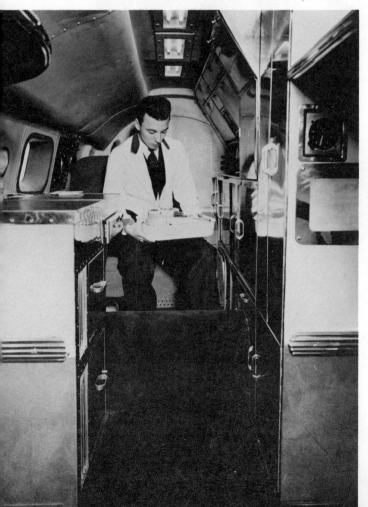

Loading mail aboard a Lancastrian aircraft for CGTAS flight to Britain, 1943-1944.

Forces overseas] have not been receiving mail regulary and quickly....It is intended that the service will take care of all air mail for the armed services, as well as carrying official passengers who may be travelling on government business." With these words the first step was taken to extend the airlines routes to cover the North Atlantic.

TCA air crews who flew this hazardous route included members of the RCAF and also the RAF acting as navigators. They flew hastily converted unarmed Avro Lancaster bombers, which later became known in airline service as Lancastrians. The machines carried their loads of passengers and mail from Dorval, Montreal, to Prestwick, Scotland. Stops were made if weather was bad, or mechanical conditions dictated, at Gander, Newfoundland, or Goose Bay, Labrador, as well as Iceland if necessary. These aircraft in search of a welcome landfall were unpressurized, which made flying uncomfortable for both passengers and crew.

The first TCA Lancaster to fly across the Atlantic roared down the runway at Dorval on 22 July 1943 with Captain Ron George, TCA's Operation's Manager at its controls. The machine also carried three passengers—Mr. W. Houston, Superintendent of de Havilland Aircraft plant, J.R.K. Main, Inspector of Airways, Department of Transport, and C.S. Ritchie, of the Department of External Affairs. As well as its passengers, the aircraft carried 2,600 pounds of mail, and an extra flight crew to be based in the United Kingdom to operate the return flight. The flying time for the crossing was 12

Three passengers preparing to board the first TCA Lancastrian to fly to Prestwick, Scotland, from Montreal on 22 July 1943.

The arrival in Scotland of the CGTAS flight on 23 July 1943 showing passenger being greeted by Colonel E.J. Underwood of Canadian Army HQ Overseas.

hours, 26 minutes, thereby establishing a new record for the crossing from Canada, cutting 25 minutes off the existing one.

The CGTAS would act, during its years of operation, as a valuable proving ground for TCA's future transatlantic services during the postwar years. The Lancasters flew both day and night, weather permitting. The weather over the long route to Scotland was notoriously unreliable and many of the aircraft received a severe buffeting enroute. Nowadays, Air Canada's Boeing 747s criss-cross the Atlantic with negligible discomfort for the 365 passengers on board. Passengers travelling on AC Flight 856 leave Toronto in the evening and arrive at London Airport in roughly seven hours flying time. During each flight the aircraft has flown most of the time well above the weather. The slow, lumbering Lancasters would, by comparison need almost double the time to make the crossing with little in the way of comfort for their passengers.

One particular CGTAS Lancaster making the westbound flight ran into a severe storm on its way to Dorval. Large hailstones ripped into the machine's thin metal skin, tearing vicious holes in its slim fuselage. To stop the cold air from freezing them, the crew used everything from blankets to the Captain's brand new greatcoat that he had managed to buy in Scotland to block up the holes. In spite of all these efforts, the cold Atlantic air sucked everything, including the greatcoat, out into open space.

Perhaps the passengers on these and other CGTAS flights took comfort in the fact that the Lancaster was a well-proven machine capable of taking great punishment. Their four Rolls-Royce Merlin engines were among the best power units ever built for an aircraft, including the famed Supermarine Spitfire, for which they were originally designed.

All the CGTAS flights were carefully planned to the last detail. Twenty-four hours prior to departure the captain and his flight crew would be briefed as to flight time and the weather patterns that were expected enroute. Five hours before take-off another preflight briefing was held during which the crew, consisting of two pilots, a navigator, and a wireless operator, received last weather and intelligence reports concerning the flight. It was at this time that the captain made his final decision as to whether or not the machine would depart.

The flight to Prestwick was usually made nonstop. Flying was mostly done on this route at night with celestial navigation aiding the pilots, in much the same manner as was commonly used by seamen. Radio transmission and reception, the vital link between an aircraft and the ground, was better under nighttime conditions. Nowadays, the ultra modern navigation systems fitted to the jet airliners will guide a flight right

CGTAS Lancastrian at Dorval Airport, 1944.

across the Atlantic to the arrival gate at any destination. However, even now pilots keep up with the older systems of navigation in case of any malfunction while aboard the aircraft. Air Canada pilots still learn the Morse code for the same reason.

In February 1944 Mr. J.H. Cooper of RAF Transport Command Passenger Service flew on a TCA flight from Prestwick to Dorval. He later wrote a story concerning his experiences for the airline's house publication, *Between Ourselves.* The following passages are taken from his story, and show something of the conditions shared by both the passengers and crew during the long haul across the Atlantic:

It's chocks away at 12:00 noon British Standard Time and a few minutes after take-off we're over the sea, and the shoreline is vanishing into the distance behind us. Now we are out of sight of all land, and settling down to a ten hour flight over the sea. The aircraft starts to gain altitude, and as we go up, the oxygen supply comes on, and the passengers are busily adjusting their oxygen masks. At 15,000 feet, Jack Frost artistically decorates the outside windows of the cabin with crystal like designs. The temperature in the cabin drops considerably, we can see our breath now, and the warm flying suits are appreciated by us all. We have conquered the cloud formation at 26,500 feet. The Lancaster's four mighty power plants still drive us forward at four miles a minute, and at this great speed, we have crossed over the weather, and are descending on the other side....Soon it was dark with the frost gone from the windows, the stars, and the moon stand out in the cold night air. Then we are over the huge airport circling the field, making our letdown, and then Captain Barclay "three-points" the big aircraft perfectly, and we roll up to the big hangar.

This flight from Prestwick had been routine and Service No. CMW—8 had carried several hundred pounds of freight plus eight passengers and 3,800 pounds of eagerly awaited forces' mail. The writer summed up his feeling in this prophetic way: "And so it goes on—day after day—modern aircraft providing swift air transportation, conquering space, spanning oceans, and linking continents—yes, making history, and a better world tomorrow."

The Canadian Government Transatlantic Air Service proved a great success, and the first three aircraft used on it were literally pulled off the assembly line at the Victory Aircraft plant at Malton, Ontario, to be converted from their role as bombers and modified for TCA freight and passenger duties. By the end of 1945 the service had

TCA aircrew being presented with a gift for having flown the Atlantic more than one hundred times. Note the RCAF officer who was part of the crew. This event took place in 1945..

changed from its quasi-military style to that of a civilian airline. From its commencement in 1943 the CGTAS had made five hundred crossings of the Atlantic. The company would add another six hundred crossings to its existing record the following year.

Late in 1945 TCA opened its first London office. The transatlantic fare at the time was $675 for the round trip. The service prepared the way for Air Canada's overseas operations during the postwar years. As Graham Nettleton, who was the wireless operator aboard TCA's first Atlantic flight, said later, "We flew at 17,000 or 18,000 feet and had to wear oxygen masks. The aircraft's heaters were right beside my seat, and when the Captain called for more heat the perspiration dripped off my nose."

By early 1945 TCA was making active plans for its postwar expansion. During the war period the company had increased its transcontinental schedule to three flights a day, and was encouraging Canadians to think of Canada as being an air-minded country. The pattern of development planned by TCA at this time also included better service to the Pacific Coast and the prairies by providing them with what amounted to a third aerial highway across the rest of the country. This was accomplished with the opening of a third daily service across the country, which would connect with TCA's existing flight schedules on the Edmonton-Lethbridge section of the flight. Bypass services also connected Saskatoon into the system. One of the main objectives of improving the transcontinental service was to bring it up to four flights daily spaced six hours apart, providing 'round the clock operations. All TCA needed to complete these plans were additional flight crews, who would be picked from the large numbers of returning RCAF air crews.

From March 1944 to the spring of 1945 over sixty ex-RCAF pilots had graduated from TCA's instructional school at Winnipeg. The main purpose of this program was to retrain experienced pilots and absorb them into TCA for the more peaceful days ahead. These young men were all RCAF "repats," who had, up until their return to Canada, been serving with operational units in wartime Europe or other theatres of war. Many of these fliers had a large number of flying hours on multi-engined aircraft to their credit. All the pilots in the first group to be trained by TCA were qualified as first officers in 1945. Their qualifications before they had joined TCA were at least one tour of operations together with a minimum of 1,000 flying hours. Many of the pilots who took advantage of the course had up to 2,000 flying hours. The average age of these pilots was 25 years.

The company had come to an agreement with the RCAF in 1944 for the program.

TCA Lodestar flying above Canada's Pacific coast.

The techniques needed to fly the little TCA Lodestars were far different from those required aboard a Lancaster on its final bombing run over its target in Germany. So the former service pilots had to go back to ground school. Once again they used the famous Link trainer, which never left the ground, but simulated the student's pattern of flying. The course offered by TCA lasted for six weeks, with the students often putting in a ten-hour day. The reward at the end of this gruelling course was to be called into the office of the Superintendent of Flying Operations, Barney Rawson, who would hand the newly qualified TCA first officer his earphones, accompanied by a brusque hand-shake.

It was also in 1945 that TCA developed its plans for placing a four-engined airliner in its fleet. The knowledge gained during the war had pushed aircraft design ahead at a tremendous pace that would not have been possible in the prewar era. The wartime need for more powerful transport aircraft had been acute. At the end of hostilities many of the existing transport machines could be released for civilian duties.

Trans-Canada Air Lines had announced as early as November 1944 its plans to use the DC-4M1, a civilian version of the rugged troop transport built in the United States, but powered by four Rolls-Royce Merlin engines. This machine finally entered fleet service as the Canadair North Star, being assembled at the Canadair plant in Montreal. The aircraft was large in comparison with TCA's existing Lockheed machines, as the following statistics show:

	Lockheed Lodestar	Canadair DC−4M
Overall length	49'10"	93'11"
Span overall	65'6"	117'6"
Height	11'10"	27'6"
Take-off weight	19,605 lbs.	79,850 lbs.

These figures bear little comparison to those of Air Canada's 747s now in service with

"I name you North Star. May God prosper you and those who fly with you." Mrs. C.D. Howe on christening the first North Star to enter service with TCA.

North Star interior

their weight of over 400 tons unloaded. However, the first steps had been taken by TCA which would lead the airline toward the future jet age.

The company's domestic services now began to reach out to cover the country. Flying at night as a passenger within the warm cocoon of a little Lockheed was a time to reflect, as Major Gus Sivertz did on a TCA flight on Christmas Eve 1945. This is what he wrote in a story for *Between Ourselves*:

> Over the starboard wingtip, throwing gleams of cold light on the silvered metal, played the weird spectacle of the Northern Lights—the Aurora Borealis. Like a huge hand it covered the Northern horizon: now pale and chill; now brilliant as it reached to the

zenith. Like fingers of ectoplasm from a million heroic dead reaching towards heaven. And steady as a ship upon a placid sea the airliner knifed through the night sky; winging its way westward with a human cargo. The passengers were not all asleep. The tall Air Force Corporal sat bolt upright and smoked one cigarette after another as he stared straight ahead. It was a race against time, and only the speed of flight could help him to win and see his mother alive. Morning came and the fabulous sunrise of the West filled the plane with gold and flame-coloured light.

During the first few months of peace TCA made improvements to its hangars and navigational aids. Nineteen forty-five was also the year when the company's first Douglas DC–3 aircraft joined its fleet, as part of the twenty-four military transports that had been acquired from the services and converted for civil use. These renowned machines had a 21-seat capacity, and a range of 1147 miles.

Following the war's end radar, the miracle that had sought out so many enemy targets, became available for peacetime use. TCA and the RCAF had worked closely with the Department of Transport for some time to develop its peacetime use. In 1945 radar was experimented with at Winnipeg, finally going into full service in 1957, and

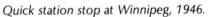

Quick station stop at Winnipeg, 1946.

34

enabled pilots to pick out the mountains or to see the movements of other airplanes in the night sky. Radar acted as the "all-seeing eye" for the operators on the ground or in the air.

Radios had also greatly improved during the war, and by June 1945, the ultra modern very high frequency (VHF) units were going into service on TCA's chain between Toronto, Ottawa, and Montreal. Radio reception and transmission in this area had always been erratic because of the hills that stood between the three centres. These natural obstacles caused static interference, and at times complete radio blackouts. Through the use of VHF units the wireless operators aboard the airliners travelling on this route experienced no interference from static conditions. TCA was the first airline to make VHF standard at all ground stations in 1945.

The LORAN Navigation System, which had been developed during the war, was a great boon to TCA crews flying the Atlantic. Now accurate fixes could be made for well over eight hundred miles during the day, and fourteen hundred miles at night. This sophisticated system could be used in all weather conditions, which was a great relief to the navigators who had to plot the aircraft's course, and who had been outfoxed so often in the past by the weather. Here again the close spirit of cooperation that existed between the RCAF and TCA made it possible for the airline to install the system.

The Loran system had been invented by an American, but his knowledge had been made available to the wartime allies, and perhaps one of the greatest benefits to man following the horrors of war was the peaceful use of radar and other navigational systems. It was from the workshops of war that our present sophisticated guidance systems were developed. By 1945 the problems caused by weather were being overcome, as "overweather" flying had become a reality.

By the beginning of January 1946 TCA's list of "Million Milers" had been compiled. This list contained all the pilots in the company who had flown over a million miles. There were twenty names, including Art Rankin, Herb Seagrim, George Lothian, Lowell Dunsmore, Ken Main, Jock Barclay, Paul Jensen and Rene Giguère and 'Lindy' Rood. The figure of a million miles gives some idea of the flying experience accumulated at the time by TCA's veteran pilots. The calculations were made by Captain Giguère by multiplying the pilots' flying hours by the average ground speed of TCA aircraft. The average speed was taken as being 166 mph for the domestic services, and 215 mph for the transatlantic route.

Captain George Lothian became the first Canadian pilot to make a hundred crossings of the Atlantic whilst a TCA captain. The long hours of Atlantic flying with CGTAS

Arrival of first group of immigrants under the Canadian government's immigration by air program at Dorval Airport, 4 June 1948.

had given TCA air crews aboard the plodding Lancasters vital experience in transoceanic flying. New names and routes had been added to TCA's expanding network, such as Kellavik, Reykjavik, Bluie West One and the Azores. In spite of some of the intriguing place names, all of them were emergency stops in mid-Atlantic, which had already proved the grim graveyard for many an aircraft and its hapless crew.

One of the main events during 1946 came in December, when one of the company's nine Lancastrians made TCA's thousandth Atlantic crossing. At this time the frequency of the CGTAS flights flown by TCA crews were matching those of the major international airlines, who were all seeking the valuable postwar Atlantic air routes. By 1946 the CGTAS aircraft were crossing the ocean on a daily basis, and six hundred flights were flown during the year without any cancellations being made. On 16th September the service was extended from Prestwick, Scotland, to London.

Nineteen forty-seven was the year the four-engined North Star went into fleet service with TCA. The first models of the North Star to be built by Canadair were unpressurized. The aircraft was to serve with TCA for many years, until finally retired from active flying in 1961. Mrs. C.D. Howe christened the first North Star while her husband, by this time Minister for Reconstruction and Supply, looked proudly on, no doubt recalling the "Dawn to Dusk flight" of the tiny Lockheed in 1937.

Some idea of TCA's growth at this time can be gained from the following figures, which cover the period from 1938 to 1946. Apart from transatlantic operations

	1938	1940	1944	1946
Passengers carried	2,086	53,180	156,884	305,442
Airmail carried	367,734 lbs	927,037 lbs	3,739,105 lbs	2,325,977 lbs.

In spite of all the technical achievements accomplished by 1946, the weather was still the pilots' real enemy, especially in the grim Canadian winter. Ice was the main hazard. New de-icing systems as well as cabin heaters were quickly put into service, and in some instances "redesign" became the watchword regarding TCA's equipment. By 1947 many of the country's existing airports had been improved, especially those that served the major centres. Radar and radio links had been expanding across Canada, and these helped to control the growing aircraft movements.

During the airline's first decade TCA had flown across both Canada and the Atlantic. The fleet's aircraft had grown more powerful. The company's officials had taken their places at the world's conference tables where organizations such as The International Air Transport Association (IATA) worked for a better understanding between the world's governments and their attitudes toward civil aviation and the airline industry. H.J. Symington, TCA's President, became President of IATA in 1945.

Trans-Canada Air Lines was firmly established as the national flag carrier in 1947. By this time the company was ready for its period of expansion in the next decade. In a statement made to the House of Commons on 2 April 1943, Canada's Prime Minister had said: "Trans-Canada Air Lines will continue to be the instrument of the government in maintaining all transcontinental air transport services and in operating services across

Hon. Lester B. Pearson enroute to the Paris conference with his wife, 29 October 1948, shown at Dorval prior to take-off.

TCA DC-3 flying over Niagara Falls, Ontario, early 1950s.

international boundary lines and outside Canada." His words echoed the thoughts of many people at TCA in the postwar era. As 1948 approached, a new age was about to open in the history of air transport; the jet engine was making its shrill voice heard as fighters streaked across the land.

Part Two

YEARS OF EXPANSION 1948–1960

Super Constellation with a North Star and two DC-3s shown at Vancouver Airport, 1954.

The problem of managing an airline can be greatly simplified if one basic rule is observed: so plan and manage that throughout the corporate history of the airline its capacity for the provision of air transportation shall, in quantity and in quality be correctly related to the transportation market to be served.

G.R. McGREGOR
President, Air Canada 1948-1968

S TRONG LEADERSHIP PROVIDES the very essence for advancement, and also gives stimulus when it is most needed. The future expansion of Trans-Canada Air Lines was assured with the appointment of Gordon R. McGregor as President in 1948. This clear-minded and dynamic man with his able team of advisors would guide the airline through the next two decades. This was the man who to literally hundreds of employees was known by his initials "G.R." On leaving McGill University he had joined the Bell Telephone Company, becoming an executive in 1938 at the company's offices in Montreal.

A native of Quebec, McGregor's first experience at the controls of an aircraft came in 1932. His natural expertise as a pilot won him the highly valued Webster Trophy, awarded annually for the best amateur pilot, for the years 1935, 1936, and 1938. His flying ability led him to join No. 115 Auxiliary Squadron RCAF. He quickly became a Flying Officer and shortly after the outbreak of war was posted overseas. He served with distinction during the Battle of Britain in 1940, and throughout the rest of the war winning the O.B.E. and D.F.C., and was finally demobilized as a Group Captain in October 1945.

McGregor joined Trans-Canada Air Lines as the company's General Traffic Manager in 1945, and some two years later he became President. He was an apt choice for the post; he had wide experience in aviation and proven ability as an administrator. He

G.R. McGregor, President of TCA, Donald Gordon, President of CNR and Grant McConachie, President of CPAL enroute to Vancouver, 31 January 1952.

Servicing TCA North Star at Gander, Newfoundland.

was a practical, down-to-earth man, who could express his opinion when necessary without beating about the bush.

In spite of the fact that traffic both domestically and internationally was high, 1948 was in many ways a difficult year for the airline. Two new overseas routes were added that year to the company's network: to Bermuda and the British West Indies. Trans-Canada Air Lines now had a new branch, Trans-Canada Air Lines (Atlantic), formed on 7 May 1947, when the airline took over control of the Canadian Government Transatlantic Air Service to the United Kingdom. Even with the prospect of increased traffic, labour costs, the need to place four-engined aircraft in service, and the costs of much-needed supplies caused concern. It was also clear that the North Atlantic route would lose money at the start, even though in future years it became an important foundation of TCA's international operations as their gateway to continental Europe.

During 1948, the forty-passenger Canadair North Star flew on the company's do-

A TCA North Star arriving at Montreal from Europe, 1948.

mestic routes. In 1947 TCA purchased twenty-three of them at a cost of $700,000 each to replace the veteran Lancastrians on the Atlantic route. The North Stars were spacious aircraft for their day and provided greater passenger comfort for long distance flights. The later types were pressurized, which made the discomfort of wearing oxygen masks at high altitudes a thing of the past. The North Star program helped the Canadian aviation industry to overcome the postwar depression caused by the completion of wartime requirements. The new airlines also made it possible for the North Stars to be put on mainly inter-city routes beginning May 1, 1948.

Severe flooding in British Columbia in 1948 put an added strain on TCA's man-power and resources. Eleven thousand people and 600,000 pounds of mail and much-needed supplies were airlifted during the first three weeks of the emergency with six flights a day being made by TCA aircraft alone. Delays in regular flight schedules were caused through these necessary relief operations, which occurred just as the company was placing new aircraft in service.

In this year also, the Canadian government instituted an airmail service whereby all letters or packages weighing under an ounce would be sent by first-class airmail at the

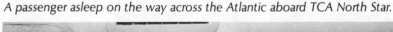

A passenger asleep on the way across the Atlantic aboard TCA North Star.

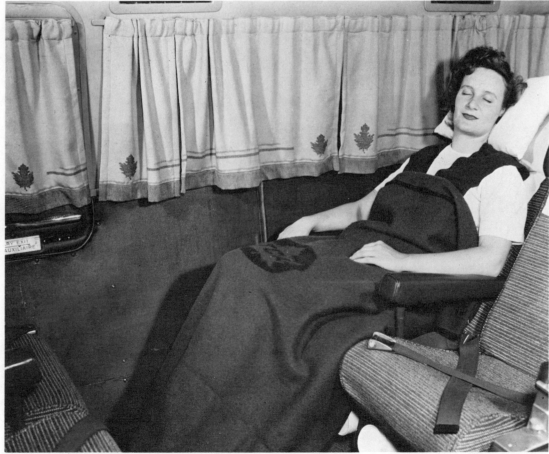

Loading a DC-3 at Yarmouth, Nova Scotia, after 1949; note the cargo.

regular postage rates. Canada was the first country in the world to offer such a service; at the time she had the least expensive airmail service in the world.

Nineteen forty-nine marked the appearance of the controversial Avro Jetliner, the first jet transport to be built in North America. The machine had been produced in co-operation with the company's British counterpart and the Hawker Siddeley group. Work had been completed by Avro (Canada) and the fifty-seat Jetliner, powered by four Rolls-Royce Derwent 5 engines made its first official flight at Malton on 10 August just two weeks after the unveiling of the British-built de Havilland Comet. Flight and proving tests were carried out on the Avro Jetliner for over a year, during which time an airmail flight was made by the aircraft to New York. From the time it first flew, this Canadian machine had put the nation into active competition with aircraft companies in the United States who were racing ahead with their designs for the future Boeing and Douglas airliners. The world market was ready for the first jet airliners, which had been made possible by earlier designs for the jet fighters, flown during the latter part of the Second World War. TCA was highly interested therefore in the development of the Avro Jetliner, designated the C-102.

Mr. F.W. Crickard, TCA's three millionth passenger, receiving a souvenir of the occasion at Dorval Airport, 25 July 1950.

46

Captain Bob Smith being interviewed at Orly Airport, Paris, having made the TCA inaugural service to France, 1 April 1951.

Unfortunately for its Canadian manufacturer the Jetliner's air-frame design was not greatly changed from that of the conventional propeller-driven aircraft. Many airlines around the world were also eagerly waiting to see what would happen to the British-designed Comet, one of the most graceful airplanes ever produced, and years ahead of its time in design. Therefore, the airlines waited before placing firm orders with the Canadian company, and finally the decision had to be taken to cancel the plans for the Avro Jetliner. It was a sad thing for Canada, because the jet age was fast approaching, and this move left the North American field wide open to the Boeing and Douglas designs. One of the most dramatic events in this period was the unveiling of the Soviet-built Tupolev TU-104, which appeared even before the Americans had got their prototypes into production.

At the beginning of 1950 TCA had a staff of 4,904. By this time many more of the pilots had flown a million miles. Once again the resources of the company were pushed to their limit for an emergency situation. In May of that year the Red River around Winnipeg had overflowed its banks. For five days from May 8 to 13, TCA flew forty special round-trip flights between Winnipeg and Eastern Canada. Relief supplies carried in the company's aircraft amounted to 500,000 pounds of badly needed materials and during those dangerous days 2,500 people were evacuated from the flooded areas.

Because of increasing demands for all types of air transport in 1951, TCA felt the need for better airports and facilities both for its passenger and for its mail and cargo operations. On 1 April TCA's overseas flights were extended to include Paris. This was the start of a period of increased emigration from Europe, still recovering from the aftermath of war. In particular, many immigrants were coming from the British Isles to

TCA North Star with its waiting load of cargo, 1952.

TCA Super Constellation at Dusseldorf Airport, 1954, 1955.

start life anew in this Commonwealth country. The airline flew 644 flights across the North Atlantic, all of them in the rugged North Stars. These sturdy machines proved their reliability again and again, in spite of complaints by some of the crew about noise and vibration. The North Star was not a favourite aircraft with a number of pilots, but its four-engine capability was a boon on the Atlantic runs.

Nevertheless, TCA was actively searching for more powerful aircraft with greater capacity and the range for both transcontinental and transatlantic routes. The Lockheed Constellation had been flying successfully with airlines around the world and had a proven record. The Super Constellation could carry between sixty and seventy passengers in comfort. With its four engines, it had an operating range greater than that of the North Star and a cruising speed of 310 mph as compared to the North Star's 230 mph. TCA placed its first order for five of these machines to be delivered to the company in 1953.

To meet the needs of an expanding air cargo market that was now handling almost anything from highly perishable moose meat to heavy equipment, in 1953 TCA added to its fleet three extremely durable aircraft, the Bristol Type 170 MK 31, known around the world as the Freighter or Wayfarer. The machine, with its fixed undercarriage, was a high-winged monoplane ungainly in appearance, with enormous nose doors that when opened gave it a voracious look. Because of its powerful Bristol Hercules engines, this oddly old-fashioned looking machine could fly almost anywhere, often landing in conditions that would have been impossible for any other type of aircraft. It had a gross weight of 44,000 pounds and rather sluggish cruising speed of 165 mph, which earned it the reputation as the "tramp steamer" of the airways. However, its flying habits endeared it to pilots. The British-designed twin-engined aircraft had first flown in 1945 and had been purchased by a growing number of air carriers. During the 1948 Berlin airlift Bristol Freighters had carried in thousands of pounds of supplies. TCA acquired its Freighters from Bristol and finally retired them in 1955. These

TCA cargo aircraft being loaded with a shipment of chicks bound for Lima, Peru.

TCA's Bristol Freighters Mk 31 at Malton. These aircraft proved to be very useful to the airline for cargo operations, 1953.

lumbering aircraft are still flying in service around the world. One of the airline's Bristol airplanes bearing the registration letters CF—TFX flew to the barren polar region in 1967, before landing at the true North Pole. Today the same aircraft in Wardair colours is mounted on a pedestal at Yellowknife as a lasting memorial to the aerial wayfarers who plod their unglamorous paths across the northern skies. Specially converted Canadair North Stars took the place of the redoubtable Bristol Type 170 in TCA's cargo service during 1954.

As far as TCA was concerned, 1954 could be called the year of the Constellation, for it was at this time the long-awaited machine went to service, cutting two hours off the transcontinental flight alone. Its arrival released North Stars for domestic and cargo purposes. The latter had been in continuous use and the need for a replacement aircraft had become urgent. The flood of immigrants was gathering momentum, and it was becoming apparent that air transport was rapidly replacing the traditional sea crossing for more and more families.

In 1955 TCA caused quite a stir in North America when it became the first airline to introduce turbo-prop aircraft into its fleet. This was the elegant Vickers Viscount, a British-made machine that had already made a considerable impact on commercial aviation. The Viscount was well received in Canada, and soon became a favourite with passengers and crew alike. It would be in both TCA and Air Canada service for many

Inaugural Super Constellation "Pacific Mercury" nonstop Toronto-Vancouver, 26 September 1954. The RCAF band in the foreground is from the Supply Depot, Downsview, Ontario.

(Photo courtesy Transport Canada)

Toronto Airport, 1956. General view the facilities; note the position of the runways.

years to come before being retired in 1974. The Viscounts started flying on the TCA route between Montreal and Winnipeg on 1 April 1955. Later the same month they began operating to New York, the first time this ultra-modern turbo-prop had been seen in the United States in the service of a commercial airline.

By the end of 1955 TCA was flying a route network of 23,714 miles, which included destinations in Canada and the United States as well as a host of other countries from Bermuda to continental Europe. Eighteen years previously TCA had an initial route structure of just 122 miles.

Any airline wishes to operate in a prosperous climate, and by 1956 the buoyant Canadian economy provided a stimulus for the nation's air carrier. In this year two million passengers were carried, and over a billion passenger miles were flown by the company's aircraft. In this year of the Hungarian Revolution, TCA brought a steady stream of refugees to this country aboard its scheduled and specially chartered flights. These people coming to Canada in search of a new life were transported by the company, which was also instrumental in delivering many tons of emergency and relief supplies to Europe to meet the vital requirements of the international relief organizations.

Just twenty years after the company's formation another historic event took place with TCA's inauguration of a nonstop service between Toronto and Vancouver. The Lockheed Super Constellations were able to cut the flying time to seven hours, less than half the time needed for the transcontinental flight in 1939. There were now seven daily flights to the West Coast. By the end of 1957 TCA was serving fifty-six communities in Canada, thirty-nine of which had a total population of under 100,000 people. Later the same year, on 29 September, a nonstop service was begun across the Atlantic from Toronto. During the busy summer months up to twelve flights flew over the route in both directions.

An order worth $67,000,000 was placed by TCA for the Vickers Vanguard, which could well be described as the bigger brother of the graceful Viscount. This was to be the largest single dollar order ever placed in postwar Britain. The Vanguards would eventually fly on routes not suited to the shorter-range Viscounts or the long-range Douglas DC−8s, that would soon become a part of TCA's expanding fleet.

In 1958 the company once more showed its usefulness in a crisis, when all surface transport between Vancouver Island and the mainland was temporarily cut. TCA began an emergency airlift, and in a five-day period carried 11,500 passengers on 350 flights, proving once again the company's ability to provide essential passenger service.

By 1959 air travel was becoming so popular that the TCA/CNR credit card was introduced, enabling businessmen and women in particular to use the services of both rail and air routes. The year also saw the completion of a program installing all-weather radar on TCA's Super Constellations and Vickers Viscounts. The airline's fleet at the end of 1959 stood at thirteen Super Constellations, forty-nine Vickers Viscounts, twenty-one Canadair North Stars, and nine DC–3s. The company's huge new maintenance base at Dorval was nearing completion. These facilities would provide accommodation for the new generation of jet aircraft.

In 1937 few of the passengers carried on those early TCA flights could have realized as they ate their boxed lunches and made so many stops en route that it would be possible to travel aboard a TCA aircraft in complete comfort only occasionally feeling the force of adverse weather conditions that had so often caused discomfort during the early days. Full meal service was an everyday event in 1959 aboard aircraft belonging to the international airlines, especially those flying across the highly competitive North Atlantic route. The liners that still ploughed their sedate passage across the

Toronto International Airport (Malton); general view under winter conditions showing terminal building, 1959.

A McDonnell Douglas DC-8 destined for TCA under construction.

(Photo courtesy Douglas Airport Company)

ocean reached Montreal in five days, whilst the airliners flying high above them made the flight in just a few hours. A vital change had taken place and air transport was now reaching out to encompass what would later be so aptly termed the "global village." From 1948 to 1959 a dream which far-sighted people had had so many years before was fast being realized: Canada now had her own modern, national airline.

By careful planning and management TCA was getting ready to bring into service its first jet airliners. Even in 1959 such aircraft were still regarded with a sense of wonder, as TCA edged up to the approaching jet age.

1. Baggage being loaded on DC-8
2. Air Canada handles many types of freight, including cattle
3. Stretched version of DC-8 in hangar
4. Last-minute fuel check
5. DC-9 in flight
6. DC-9 in flight
7. Big birds at rest

1

2

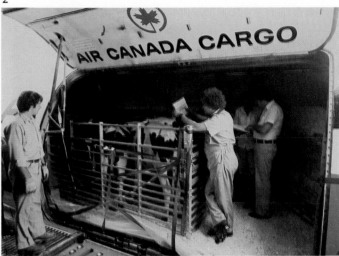

3

4

5

6

7

9

8

10

8. Containerized cargo being
   loaded aboard Boeing 747
9. Boeing 747 near departure
   time
10. Cockpit check before take
    off

11. Boeing 747. The wing span
    is 196 feet
12. Boeing 747 prior to lift-off
13. Ground handling of
    containerized cargo

12

11

13

14

15

16

17

18
19

20

21. Passengers checking for
    departure at ticket counter
22. Final briefing for flight crew
23. First officer checking
    engine and fuel gauges
24. "Would you like a
    magazine, sir?"

21

22

23

24

THE JET AGE   1960-1977

Front view of Boeing 747 showing ground-handling crew. Note the tug used to tow the massive aircraft.

*In the next forty years, the development of the (airline)
industry may be so breathtaking as to make the first forty
years seem slow.*

CLAUDE I. TAYLOR
General Manager Marketing Services, now President of Air Canada.

IN 1960 TCA'S first Douglas DC–8 jet airliner went into operation. This powerful aircraft, capable of carrying its load of 133 passengers at a speed of more than 550 mph, was powered by four Rolls-Royce Conway engines. With its arrival modern technology had made it possible for the aircraft to span Canada nonstop. Flying at an operational altitude of between 30,000 and 35,000 feet, the DC–8 was equipped with the most up-to-date navigational and radar devices. During the first few months the sleek jet shared the spotlight with the company's older Constellations and rugged North Stars. TCA's first Douglas DC–8 was delivered from the Douglas plant in California by Captain George Lothian, one of the company's veteran pilots on 7 February 1960. The transcontinental jet service began on 1 April, when the trip across Canada was made in just over five hours.

On 1 June 1960 the DC–8s began flying on TCA's international routes. The flying time from Montreal to London was dramatically reduced from 11 hours 10 minutes to just six hours. The streamlined new jet stood out in contrast to the remaining North Stars, as if it was a symbol of the future. In truth the Douglas DC–8 signalled the end of an era in air transport, for now the familiar propellers were being replaced by jet engines.

But the coming of the jet engine in regular international flights was not without its problems, especially in its effect on ground systems. Air traffic control, for example, had

Mr. J.A.D. McCurdy and Capt. George Lothian after the pilot of the famous Silver Dart had flown on a jet in January 1960.

TCA aircraft shown at Dorval Airport (left to right: Douglas DC-8, Vickers Vanguard, Vickers Viscount).

G.R. McGregor and G.W.G. McConachie following the announcement of TCA's and CPAL's agreement on North American fare structures, 1961.

The opening of TCA's new engineering and maintenance base at Montreal. The project cost $20 million and was opened on 15 December 1960, by the Hon. Leon Balcer, Minister of Transport.

First TCA Vickers Vanguard under construction, 31 March 1960 (Photo courtesy Vickers Aircraft Company).

long catered to propeller-driven aircraft. The jet engine had almost doubled the speed of most existing commercial aircraft, and airport runways and other facilities had to cater to the growing numbers of jets. It was a long step from TCA's ten-seat Lockheeds, that were in service in 1937 to the new generation of jet aircraft of the sixties.

By 1960 TCA had become a world airline in every sense of the word. Its fleet flew on both short-haul and long-distance flights in Canada and the United States, linking the larger trading and industrial centres together and reaching to a multitude of small communities in North America. Its many international flights linked Canada with destinations that varied from the Caribbean to Europe. Airports in Canada now differed greatly from those grass fields of the 1930s where a few curious onlookers had watched the sporadic arrivals and departures of the small airliners. Now some of the larger terminals were assuming the size of small towns as their mass of passengers and staff went about the business of air transport.

The company's massive new maintenance base at Dorval was completed in 1961 and covered eighty-four acres. This huge structure was geared from the start to meet the needs of the larger aircraft, especially the modern jets. The year also saw the withdrawal from service of the veteran North Stars. The Douglas DC–8s were put into intensive use during the summer; a total of 2,600 seats were available for the transatlantic flights, and 508 seats daily in each direction across Canada.

Gradually the few remaining Constellations and North Stars were replaced by aircraft such as the powerful Vickers Vanguard, which carried a load of ninety-six passengers at a speed of 465 mph. The final North Star flight took place on 30 June 1961, fourteen years after they had replaced TCA's aging Lancastrians. In spite of its shortcomings, this enduring aircraft had proved to be a reliable machine in the postwar years.

When TCA celebrated its silver jubilee in 1962 its staff had reached 11,719, in comparison to a payroll of 71 people in 1937. Some 18,862,000 tons of airmail were carried aboard TCA's aircraft that historic year. On 7 July 1962 Her Majesty the Queen Mother flew from London to Montreal aboard one of TCA's scheduled flights.

Her majesty the Queen Mother arriving at Dorval Airport, 7 June 1962.

By 1963, which also marked a landmark in the company's history when the last propeller-driven Douglas DC–3s were phased out, TCA became the first Canadian carrier with an all-turbine fleet. By this time TCA was the ninth largest carrier in the free world. During the year the company carried a total of 3,966,547 passengers on its scheduled and charter flights. A mixed passenger/cargo version of the DC–8 flew on the Atlantic service. Also the first of the airline's DC–8F freighter aircraft went into operation in October 1963. These fast jets began a regular service between Montreal, Toronto, Winnipeg, Edmonton, and Vancouver. These machines were strictly working aircraft with no frills; they could carry a load of 45,000 lbs, and allowed a nonstop cargo flight to be made from London, England, to Vancouver, British Columbia. It was now possible to transport valuable cargoes from the British Isles to Canada's Pacific coast in one day. The freight carried aboard the jet freighters varied from livestock to perishable foods or materials.

During 1964 the company placed an order with the Douglas Aircraft Company for

Lockheed 10A CF-TCA, the first aircraft to be purchased by TCA from its manufacturer being readied by Air Canada for presentation to the National Museum in Ottawa, 1968. Note the comparative size of the DC-8 in the background.

Refurbished TCA Lockheed 10A at Toronto International Airport on its cross-Canada flight to celebrate the airline's twenty-fifth anniversary in 1962.

(Photo Courtesy Douglas Aircraft Company)

McDonnell Douglas DC-8F Jet Trader. These aircraft first entered TCA service in 1963.

eight of its DC−9s, a short to medium-haul jet airliner. Apart from benefiting the airline, these machines provided a tremendous boost to the Canadian aircraft industry, as the $65 million order stipulated that half the airframes would be built in Canada. Under this program nearly two thousand jobs were provided for Canadians.

Throughout 1964 the airline carried out a number of special flights. These included providing transportation for the Olympic Games being staged in Tokyo. On 3 October a DC−8 belonging to TCA made a record return flight from Japan to Montreal in 12 hours, 24 minutes. The same aircraft had carried Canada's official Olympic Team to Tokyo.

It was also in 1964 that Trans-Canada Air Lines and its nearest rival, Canadian Pacific Air Lines, agreed to a policy of selling "Canada first." Through this mutual agreement each company promoted the other's services as an alternate to its own. This proved to be a wise move. Intense competition was no longer necessary with the steadily growing market in international and domestic air transport.

On 13 October a DC−8 aircraft bore the company's new name, "Air Canada," for the first time. This machine carried Queen Elizabeth II aboard it for the flight from

Air Canada Vickers Vanguard taking off, 1965.

Ottawa to London, England. The change of name from Trans-Canada Air Lines to Air Canada became official on 1 January 1965 by Act of Parliament. The main reason for both the change of title and the unveiling of the new bright red Maple Leaf symbol was to better describe Canada's national airline and its international character. A number of people were not happy with the change, especially when the year celebrated the twenty-fifth anniversary of TCA's first flight across Canada in 1939. Many of these people had served with the airline since its early days and felt it was not right to break with the traditions and patterns of service established over those years. However, the traditional Maple Leaf design that had been placed on TCA's first little Electra still remained on the newer aircraft.

Between 1965 and 1966 Air Canada's traffic operations continued to increase, with new cargo terminals being opened in Toronto and completed in Vancouver. By the end of 1965 the airline's route network totalled 42,343 miles. The rivalry that existed during the period between both international and domestic carriers was having a stimulating effect on the industry. On 1 November 1966 Air Canada became the first North American airline to fly to the Soviet Union. The flight from Montreal to Moscow, via Copenhagen, allowed passengers to use Denmark as a gateway to Scandinavia and other eastern routes in Europe. The massive Soviet airline Aeroflot added Canada to its many destinations around the world.

The spirit and success of Expo made 1967 a boom year for Air Canada. The airline flew thousands of people to Montreal, and through its services introduced hundreds of Canadians to parts of the country they had not visited before. Passengers descended on Montreal and other centres, far exceeding the numbers of any previous years. The main terminal airports were strained to capacity as the steadily swelling crowds of arriving and departing passengers were joined by hundreds of others come to meet them or to say goodbye. The figures for the busy summer of 1967 showed only too clearly that vast improvements would have to be made to airports, ground facilities, and air traffic control centres in the coming years to meet the needs of the travelling public. It was fitting that Expo 67 with its spirit of international challenge and achievement should also mark the thirtieth anniversary of Air Canada.

The Douglas DC–9s joined the Air Canada fleet on 24 April 1966. This aircraft was the centre of controversy several years before, when there was pressure to purchase the French-built Caravelle aircraft, but after much political manoeuvering the company remained firm in its decision to buy the new Douglas machines. This decision was taken because of its merit and the work it would provide for the Canadian aircraft industry, and also because Douglas could offer quicker and more standardized service for spare

Night scene at Montreal International Airport, 1970.

parts. The end of the Expo Year showed Air Canada with an all-turbine fleet of 101 aircraft.

G.R. McGregor, the President of Air Canada who had guided the airline through its rapid period of change for the previous two decades, retired in 1968. G.R. had seen propeller-driven aircraft replaced by sleek, streamlined jets often flying at double the speed of conventional machines. Yves Pratte became Air Canada's Chairman and Chief Executive Officer and J.R. Baldwin became President. During G.R.'s last year in office Air Canada had generated $387 million in revenue and carried 6.5 million passengers, which in itself was a fitting tribute to G.R. McGregor.

On 25 April 1971, Air Canada introduced its gargantuan 747s into service. These 365-passenger aircraft cost $23 million each in 1971. In spite of their tremendous price and size, the new machines had a longer range making it possible to carry larger loads of passengers and cargo at jet speeds. The new giants flew with Air Canada for the first time on a nonstop flight between Toronto and Vancouver; they were later to serve the Montreal–Paris route.

These now familiar aircraft that daily fly across the world's vast expanse of airways seemed an immense size in 1971, when compared to the Douglas DC–8s Series 41:

	DC-8	Boeing 747.
Wing span:	142'4"	195'8"
Length:	150'9"	231'4"
Fuel volume:	19,170 Imp. Gals.	40,000 Imp. Gals.
Passengers:	133	365
Range:	4,800 stat miles.	more than 5,000 stat miles.
Max landing weight:	194,000 pounds	564,000 pounds.
Cruising speed:	550 mph	approx 600 mph

The Boeing 747 is equipped with the latest autopilot and navigational systems, and handles with the ease of a modern sophisticated fighter aircraft. Air Canada's 747s tower above the ordinary airliners; the 'tug' used to tow the 747 while on the ground weighs 155,000 pounds as compared to the weight of a fully loaded Vickers Vanguard of 146,000 pounds. In order to clean the 747 pilots' windshield a man would have to climb the equivalent of the height of a three-storey building. The captain sitting on the left-hand side of the 747's cockpit, would be at the same level as if he were sitting on top of a DC−9's tail. The dimensions of this jumbo jet would have allowed the redoubtable Wright brothers to have made their first flight within the 747's fuselage, which is roughly the length of a large football field. A man of average height can stand upright in the 747's main fuel tanks, which hold 40,000 Imperial gallons.

Accommodations aboard the new jumbo jet provide a standard of comfort that would have been the envy of the passengers aboard the little Lockheed Electra in 1937. The space allotted the sixteen cabin attendants aboard an Air Canada 747 would accommodate a full load of passengers and crew flying aboard a TCA Lockheed 10A airliner. The 747 in 1971 could carry 365 passengers and a load of 40,000 pounds of freight.

An Air Canada Boeing 747 being scrubbed clean.

The advent of the 747 opened the age of the "spacious jet" that is capable of carrying passengers for thousands of miles. Yet the first of the jumbo jets only made its original test flight on 9 February 1969, taking off from Boeing's Paine Field, Washington—not far from Seattle, where TCA had made their first Electra service in 1937. The giant 747 was airborne in seconds with its three-man flight crew at the controls. Jack Waddell took his position in the captain's seat with a Canadian, Brian Wygle, acting as co-pilot and Jess Wallick sitting at the flight engineer's panels in front of its rows of gleaming dials and instruments. The Boeing 747 felt like a truly classic aircraft as it rode the skies on that first test flight.

To allow the 747 project crews to have some idea as to how the machine would handle on the ground while taxiing prior to actually test-flying in the air, a simulated 747's cockpit had been mounted on a platform above a truck the same height above the tarmac as the actual cockpit. This truck was then manoeuvred along the runway controlled by the pilots sitting in the cockpit. This experiment proved invaluable for the crew to get the feel of the big plane. Never before in the story of aviation had there been an airliner to match the 747 in size.

Today, Air Canada's Boeing 747s have a flight crew of three, the captain sitting in the traditional left-hand seat with the first officer sitting to his right. The second officer, also a well-trained jet pilot, takes the flight engineer's duties aboard the aircraft. The 747 has a mass of over four hundred instruments, among them the airspeed indicator, artificial horizon indicator, altimeter, radio direction finder, and compass. The numerous instrument checks that have to be made before an Air Canada 747 leaves the ground can take up to forty-five minutes to complete. The electrical power generated through the 747's intricate mass of control and other systems gives enough current to light a town of five thousand people. The machines are equipped with the latest sophisticated and computerized INS (Inertial Navigation System) equipment, which guides the jet from its moment of take-off to its arrival gate at its destination.

To meet the inflight needs of today's passengers, service aboard an Air Canada 747 includes full-course meals; drinks are also served enroute. The aircraft's cabin crew generally consists of a flight director and as many as eleven flight attendants, plus a purser and his two assistants. The flight director is in charge of the cabin crew during the flight. To while away the time current movies are shown. Many of the working conditions aboard today's jumbo jets would have been the envy of a lone stewardess aboard a Lockheed Electra forty years ago.

There is little need to worry about weather conditions aboard a 747 travelling at

32,000 feet at a cruising speed of 570 mph, because the craft is guided through every phase of its flight. Radar alone enables the captain to see for up to a hundred miles ahead, so that usually the aircraft can literally fly around the bad weather spots. Far beneath the aircraft flying on the international routes over the oceans weather ships continually check the changing patterns of the weather systems. At airports sophisticated air traffic control systems are often capable of indicating by radar the position of every aircraft in the air within a radius of up to 120,000 square miles.

To keep the standards of airline safety as high as possible many international carriers, including Air Canada, make use of simulators on the ground to provide valuable added training and upgrading for their pilots who are going on to new aircraft. Air Canada maintains flight simulators for its main types of aircraft such as the Boeing 747. Through their computerized nerve centres these devices can simulate anything that might actually occur in the air, and also any ground conditions that might have to be contended with at an airport such as Toronto International. On a wide screen in front of the two pilots, runway and approach lights flicker, and the crew can feel every movement. Emergencies, such as cockpit fires or the loss of engine power, can provide valuable experience, which could never be obtained in flight. To operate an Air Canada Boeing 747 simulator costs $500 an hour, and the flight time is officially logged for the crews. Most of the simulators now in use for a variety of Air Canada aircraft were built in Montreal by CAE, and every detail in the flight control and other systems is faithfully duplicated in them.

In-flight service is especially important on long distance flights, and in keeping with the other ranking airlines, TCA and then Air Canada have done their best to help their passengers. In the mid 1940s passengers often grew bored with a flight, which might last twelve hours or more across the Atlantic. Today the same flight would take just over seven hours to complete. One way the passengers like to while away the time is by eating and drinking. Aboard the Lockheed 14 it was impossible to serve anything other than cold cuts or sandwiches together with coffee poured from a king-sized thermos, which must have been the bane of any stewardess at the time. In the narrow interior of the twelve-passenger Lancastrian the meals were served by the steward, who had to nimbly cross a two-foot high wing spar to reach his tired passengers. By today's standards the meals would seem to be austere, consisting of soup and steaming casseroles heated in the aircraft's tiny galley.

When the North Star entered TCA service quick-frozen dishes were added to the menus on the long transatlantic route. On the outbound trip the aircraft usually travelled Northward via Gander, Newfoundland or Goose Bay, Labrador. The outbound flight would fly westward via Iceland, or possibly the Azores and Bermuda. On these lengthy flights the passengers had to be provided with two meals. During this time an innovation was made by the airline, when meal vouchers were sold at prices varying from 35¢ to $1.50. An afternoon snack included cold chicken, potato salad, rolls and butter.

TCA started its bar service in 1947: on the transatlantic route prior to this only coffee or cold drinks had been served. In 1957 bar service was extended to include the West Indies and New York, because TCA was in active competition with the American carriers on these routes. It was not until 1966 that alcohol could be served to passengers on the domestic routes. Today the wines and spirits carried on board long-range flights by Air Canada could be favourably compared to those served on the ground in a first-class restaurant.

By 1949 it was possible to serve special foods on TCA airliners, including diabetic menus and Kosher food, as well as meals for salt-free diets. During one period box lunches complete with chocolate bars were prepared for children on a purely experimental basis. However, parents soon requested that full course meals be served for children. Air Canada's in-flight service today provides gourmet meals to its first-class passengers. In the economy section the meals have fewer frills, but usually consist of either beef or chicken for the main course.

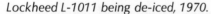

Lockheed L-1011 being de-iced, 1970.

The first Lockheed L-1011 TriStar to be bought by Air Canada being painted in the airline's colours. (Photo courtesy Lockheed Aircraft Corporation)

Mrs. Des Borrie (née Desilits) joined Air Canada in 1952 and served as a stewardess aboard most of the types of aircraft in service, including the DC–8s. She recalls: "In the 1950s you could really get to know most of your passengers on the long distance flights, and gradually a rapport grew with them. Emergencies could be dealt with by the stewardesses because they were all qualified registered nurses. The whole cabin crew performed an important public relations function for the company during the flight. In 1955 we were often working up to twenty hours on an international flight compared to an average of ten hours now." TCA's stewardesses might spend between three to five days waiting for a return flight to Canada in a city such as London. During this time the cabin crew and the flight crew really got to know each other. TCA at this time was still very much a family; most people either knew each other or about each other through contacts in various parts of Canada. Today the cabin crew might spend only one night at their overseas destination before flying back to Canada.

In 1972 Air Canada cancelled its options on the supersonic Anglo-French Concorde. This was a blow to the advocates of this aircraft, which many think is ahead of its time in aviation history. On 15 March 1973 the Lockheed TriStar L–1011 commenced service on the Toronto–Vancouver route. On 30 April Air Canada started its Rapidair service between Montreal and Toronto using Douglas DC–8s and 9s. During peak hours departures for either city were made on a half hourly basis. This special service enabled passengers to take a morning flight, complete their business, and fly back the same evening to Montreal or Toronto. After a few initial problems, service was speeded up in both cities through the use of specially designated departure gates. Jet service became available for centres in Northern Ontario. During 1973 Air Canada carried a total of 8,359,000 passengers. New all-cargo services were started, including those to Los Angeles and Copenhagen. Four cargo and two mixed cargo/passenger DC–8s provided nine freight and nine combination flights a week to Europe, and Air Canada provided another nineteen weekly freight flights across Canada. Containerization had also vastly improved, resulting in fewer losses and speedier cargo delivery for air freight to the larger centres.

After nearly twenty years in flight for both TCA and Air Canada, the last of the Vickers Viscounts were phased out of the airline's fleet in April 1974. In the following year Airtransit Canada Ltd., a subsidiary of Air Canada, started to operate an experimental STOL (short take-off/landing) service between Ottawa and Montreal, using the versatile de Havilland twenty-seat Twin Otter. These machines are capable of taking off or landing in the space of a few hundred feet. The sophisticated Canadian-built and designed machines could fly directly to downtown STOLports. During the first busy year Airtransit carried a total of 93,000 passengers. The experimental service was finally discontinued in 1975, having provided very valuable research for the future. The airline's sleek Boeing 727 jets joined the fleet the same year.

During 1975 Air Canada faced a period of strong criticism in the House of Commons by members of the opposition (Progressive Conservative) party. There were allegations concerning both improper business practices and conflict of interests in the national airline. The government immediately set up a Commission of Inquiry headed by Chief Justice Willard Estey of the Supreme Court of Ontario. The Committee worked hard during the spring and summer months of 1975, and found that no dishonesty had occurred in Air Canada's operations, but before they announced their findings Mr. Yves Pratte resigned in the belief that the government lacked confidence in his administration.

Air Canada Lockheed L-1011 flying over Montreal harbour, 1970s

72

At the beginning of 1976 Claude I. Taylor was appointed President and Chief Executive Officer of Air Canada to succeed Yves Pratte. It would be a boom year, with Air Canada achieving its first billion dollar sales year.

April 10, 1977 marked the fortieth anniversary of Air Canada, which was cele-brated by a Boeing 727 flying over the original route taken by the little Lockheed 10A four decades before to Boeing Field near Seattle, Washington. From a fleet of just three

View of Mirabel International Airport on opening day, October 1975. (Note the size of the Boeing 747 compared to the people)

tiny airplanes in September 1937 Air Canada now had a total of 120 aircraft—all jets.

Many changes have taken place during the past four decades, especially on the ground. The construction of the modern airport of Mirabel is an outstanding example. This large international terminus that opened in 1975 marked a rapid change in airport design and facilities. Although Mirabel has received its fair share of criticism, it remains one of the world's most modern airports, perhaps years ahead of its time. So far only the first phase of this operational centre has been opened, but what a different picture is presented when compared to the tiny airports of forty years ago, which in their time presented the public with an idea of modern air transport. In those days most of the airports had little in the way of control towers, and runways were almost non-existent in the modern sense of the word. Lethbridge, Alberta, had a 3,500-foot hard surface runway, which was the pride of its time. Mirabel at present has two 15,000 foot runways, each two hundred feet wide, that are capable of taking the full weight and speed

(Photo courtesy Transport Canada)

Mirabel International Airport's control tower. This structure rises 215 feet above the ground.

Mobile passenger lounges, which are driven out to the waiting aircraft at Mirabel.

of the most modern jumbo jets with their take-off weight of a maximum 710,000 pounds as compared to the little Lockheed 14's fully-loaded weight of 17,500 pounds. Mirabel's steeple-like control tower stands 215 feet above the ground, and is filled with up-to-date radar and electronic equipment with which to guide the modern airliner. During the development of the prairie route TCA worked out of the old Canadian Airways hangar in Regina—a tin building that consisted mainly of a radio room and a weather office.

Over the years, the flight paths have changed, as have the aircraft themselves. However, there are still challenges in air transport to be overcome. We will have to deal with such problems as supersonic airliners, the pollution of the airways and the noise levels of modern aircraft, problems which have international dimensions. Air traffic control must be improved, as must the levels of security against the modern menace of the aerial hijacker. All these things and many others will have to be solved in the future by the world's governments.

Today Canadians can cross their country with little discomfort. The natural barriers formed by the Rockies slip quickly beneath the wings of a modern jet airliner. The story of Air Canada reflects the achievements of a great many people who have been a part of our national airline's development and who will continue to follow the paths of Wings across Time.

Most information for this book came from Air Canada records and publications, as well as the company's Annual Reports from 1937 to 1976.

Readers who wish to pursue the subject in greater depth will find further information on the history of aviation in Canada in the following books:

David Collins. *Wings of Progress.* Toronto: Clarke Irwin, 1975

David Corbett. *Politics and the Airlines.* London: George Allen & Urwin, 1965

R.E.G. Davis. *History of the World's Airlines.* London: Oxford University Press, 1964

Frank H. Ellis. *Canada's Flying Heritage.* Toronto: University of Toronto Press, 1973

Robin Higham. *Britain's Imperial Air Routes 1918-1939.* London: Foulis, 1961

J.R.K. Main. *Voyageurs of the Air.* Ottawa: Queen's Printer, 1967

K.M. Molson. *Pioneering in Canadian Air Transport,* Winnipeg: 1974.

David Mondey, General Editor. *The International Encyclopedia of Aviation.* New York: Crown Publishers, 1977

John Stroud. *Annals of British Commonwealth Air Transport.* New York: Putnam, 1962

Georgette Vachon. *Goggles, Helmets, and Air Mail Stamps.* Toronto: Clarke Irwin, 1974

Publications:

Air International, London, England.

Canadian Aviation, Maclean-Hunter, Toronto, Canada

Flight International, London, England.

Janes *All the World's Aircraft.* Published annually since 1909, London, England.

TCA/AIR CANADA HISTORICAL HIGHLIGHTS

1937

April 10: Royal Assent was given to Bill 74 thereby creating Trans-Canada Air Lines with an authorized capital of $5 million. S.J. Hungerford of Canadian National Railways became TCA's first President (1937–1941). Don MacLaren a former First World War fighter pilot was hired from Canadian Airways.
The new airline's fleet consisted of one Stearman biplane, and two Lockheed 10As.

July 30: The historic dawn-to-dusk Trans-Canada Survey Flight was flown between St. Hubert, Quebec, and Vancouver, British Columbia. The flight, using a Lockheed 12A CF–CCT, took 17 hrs. 34 mins.

September 1: TCA made its first commercial flight from Vancouver, British Columbia to Boeing Field, Seattle, Washington.
By 31 December the company's payroll numbered 71.
By the year's end daily training flights were taking place between Winnipeg, Regina, Lethbridge and Vancouver.

1938

September 19: TCA began Air Express Services on a regular basis between Winnipeg and Vancouver.

October 1: Airmail service introduced Winnipeg—Vancouver and by December 1 reached as far as Montreal and Toronto.

TCA carried out training programs for pilots and crews, and a major repair and maintenance base was set up at Winnipeg. Night flying and instrument training were speeded up. By the end of 1938 the company's fleet was five Lockheed 10As and nine Lockheed 14Hs; the staff had increased to 332 employees.

1939

April 1: TCA made its first scheduled passenger flight between Montreal and Vancouver. Simultaneous flights were made in each direction. Service was also started between Lethbridge and Edmonton.

September: TCA went onto a war footing.

November: Airmail operations were extended to Moncton, New Brunswick. Improvements were made during the year to maintenance facilities in Montreal and Toronto. D.B. Colyer was appointed Vice-President of Operations.

1940

During the year a second transcontinental service commenced flying operations. The vice-president's and traffic headquarters were moved to Winnipeg from Montreal. Winnipeg shops enlarged to provide space for repairing instruments for military aircraft.

1941

May: H.J. Symington appointed President (1941-1947). TCA started service to New York from Toronto.
Improvements to the hangars were completed at Dorval Airport, Montreal. TCA began overhauling British Overseas Airways Corporation's aircraft, which were used on the Return Ferry Service across the Atlantic Ocean.
Lockheed Lodestars entered service with TCA. O.T. Larson became TCA's Vice-President of Operations, a post he held until 1945. At the year's end the company had 1,123 employees, including 155 women.

1942

May 1st: St. John's, Newfoundland, became part of the company's route structure. The airline's fleet stood at twenty-four aircraft, which were flying over 8,250,000 miles a year. TCA took over a new engine shop from the Department of Munitions and Supply.

1943

July 22: The company made its first transatlantic flights using unarmed Avro Lancaster aircraft. These machines were part of the Government Transatlantic Air Service. Forces' mail was carried by the Lancasters as well as passengers from Montreal, Quebec to Prestwick, Scotland.

1944

TCA flying three round trips a week between Montreal and Scotland. TCA became one of the first airlines to use oxygen for its entire fleet of unpressurized aircraft.

TCA officials attended the British Commonwealth Conference in Montreal and the World Conference in Chicago to discuss the future of Commonwealth and world air transport after the conflict. TCA's payroll now included 2,790 employees.

1945

Third daily transcontinental service started across the country. The first transatlantic passenger tickets went on sale. An air express service was also started on this route. Four additional Lancaster aircraft went into operation across the Atlantic. TCA became member of International Air Transport Association (IATA).

W.F. English became Vice-President of Operations. The 'Loran' Navigational System went into operation aboard TCA's aircraft on transatlantic service.

1946

TCA carried its one-millionth passenger.

September 16: Transatlantic service extended to London from Prestwick. TCA's fleet consisted of: twenty-seven DC–3s, fourteen Lockheed Lodestars, nine Lockheed 14s, and six Avro Lancastrians.

1947

April 30: All Canadian Government Transatlantic Air Service flights ceased; TCA officially took over the route the following day. By the year's end the company was making daily round trips across the Atlantic.

October: The first Canadair North Star (DC–4-M2) was delivered to TCA. These were the company's first fully pressurized aircraft.

1948

G.R. McGregor made President of TCA (1948-1968).

June 4: Arrival of first group of immigrants under Canadian government's immigration-by-air program, started by George Drew.

December 1: TCA started its southern service to Port of Spain, Trinidad.

1949

Headquarters Offices relocated from Winnipeg to new International Aviation Building, Montreal.

1950

April 2: Tampa, Florida, was added as stop on TCA's Caribbean service.

1951

April 1: TCA's transatlantic service extended to include Paris via London flights.

1952

May 1: Transatlantic tourist class service started.

November 5: Dusseldorf, West Germany, became part of TCA's European destinations.

1953

December 21: TCA brought Bristol Freighter 170 aircraft into service.

1954

May 14: Eight Lockheed Super Constellations entered TCA service on the Atlantic.

September 26: The Super Constellation went into service on the Montreal–Toronto–Winnipeg–Vancouver run.

1955

April 1: TCA became the first airline in North America to bring turbine-driven aircraft into service. The first of the company's 51 Vickers Viscount airliners flew on the Montreal–Toronto–Fort William (now Thunder Bay)–Winnipeg route.

1956

June 1: Toronto–Calgary nonstop services commenced using Super Constellations on the route.
During the Hungarian Revolution TCA flew refugees to Canada.

1957

September 29: TCA started Toronto–United Kingdom nonstop services.

1958

April 2:   TCA began service to Brussels.

May 15:   The airline opened service to Zurich; Montreal–Paris nonstop service started.

1959

May 1:   TCA expanded its European route to Vienna.

1960

February 7:   The first DC–8 jet aircraft was delivered to TCA.

April 1:   The DC-8 went into service on the transcontinental route.

June 1:   The DC-8 flew on the international route for the first time. The flying time from Montreal to the United Kingdom was cut from 11 hours, 10 minutes to six hours.

October: The last of the airline's North Star aircraft were withdrawn from passenger service, and the British-built Vickers Vanguard joined the Viscount.

TCA's fleet now consisted of: seven DC–8s, three Vickers Vanguards, forty-nine Vickers Viscounts, twelve Lockheed Super Constellations, twenty-one North Stars and seven DC-3s. The maintenance base was opened at Dorval Airport, Montreal.

1961

TCA's route structure covered 39,519 miles.

1962

TCA marked its first twenty-five years of operation. The airline's staff now numbered 11,719 and during the year almost 600 million ton miles of air transportation were made available.

June 7: TCA carried Her Majesty the Queen Mother from London to Montreal aboard a scheduled flight.

1963

April 12: TCA's remaining DC-3s were taken out of service, and the company became the first carrier with an all-turbine fleet.
At the year's end TCA became the ninth largest airline in the free world, and carried 3,966,547 passengers on its scheduled routes.

1964

October 3: A TCA DC–8 that had carried the Canadian Olympic Team to Japan made the nonstop return flight to Montreal in a record time of 12 hours, 24 minutes.

October 10-24: TCA operated a return charter flight between Montreal and Hamburg carrying videotapes of the Olympic Games being held in Tokyo. These tapes were later shown in nineteen European countries.

October 13: Queen Elizabeth II was flown from Ottawa to London in an Air Canada DC-8 using the company's new markings for the first time.

1965

January 1: The official change of name from Trans-Canada Air Lines to Air Canada became effective.
By the year's end Air Canada had a total route network of 42,343 miles.

1966

November 1: Air Canada became the first North American airline to fly into the Soviet Union. The route was flown from Montreal to Moscow via

Copenhagen. Aeroflot commenced its service to Canada a few days later.

1967

Expo 67 made 1967 a peak year for Air Canada, and also marked the thirtieth year of the company's founding.

April 24:   The DC-9 went into Air Canada service.

September 29:   Air Canada started direct service to Los Angeles from Montreal—Toronto.
By the year's end Air Canada's all-turbine fleet totalled 101 aircraft.

1968

May 31:   Air Canada President Gordon R. McGregor retired. Yves Pratte became Chairman and Chief Executive Officer and J.R. Baldwin President. The company generated $387.6 million, and carried over 6.5 million passengers during the year.

1969

April 1:   Air Jamaica commenced operations. Air Canada has a substantial interest in this airline owning 26.9 per cent of the shares.

1970

May 1:   Air Canada started flying into Prague in a pool service with CSA (Czechoslovak Airlines). The company's transatlantic flights now totalled forty-one services a week to the United Kingdom and twenty-nine flights to the continent.

1971

April 25:   Air Canada's Boeing 747s entered service on a daily nonstop flight between Toronto and Vancouver. During the summer months these huge aircraft also flew on the Toronto–London route, as well as the Montreal–Paris service.

October 31: The company withdrew its last Vickers Vanguard aircraft from Passenger operations.

1972

April 30: The company's Rapidair service between Montreal and Toronto was introduced.

July: Air Canada cancelled its options on the Anglo-French Concorde.

1973

March 15: The Lockheed 1011 TriStar flew for the first time on the Montreal–Vancouver route.

1974

April: The last of the company's Vickers Viscounts were withdrawn from service after nearly twenty years of operational flying.

July 24: Airtransit Canada Ltd. commenced a STOL (short take-off/landing) service between Montreal and Ottawa carrying 93,000 passengers during the year. For this operation de Havilland Twin Otters were used.

1975
Air Canada commenced its service to the French West Indies.

1976

April 30: Airtransit Canada Ltd. ceased operations.
The airline had its first billion dollar sales year.
Air Canada commenced its service to Cuba in conjunction with Cubana Airlines.

Claude I. Taylor became President and Chief Executive Officer following the resignation of Yves Pratte. P. Taschereau became Chairman of the company.

1977

September 1: The airline marked its original flight forty years previously by flying a Boeing 727 aircraft from Vancouver, British Columbia to Boeing Field, Seattle.

As of January 20, 1977, Air Canada had a fleet consisting of eight DC−8−41; six DC−8−54 (all freight); two DC−8−53; seven DC−8−61; twelve DC−8−63; forty-four DC−9−32; eight DC−9−15; one DC−9−32F; five Boeing 747−133; one Boeing 747−233; twelve Lockheed 1011; fourteen Boeing 727−233, for a total fleet of 120.

Throughout its history Air Canada has maintained a safety record of which they can be proud. However there have been some tragedies including the following:

6 February 1941   A TCA Lockheed aircraft crashed at Armstrong, Ontario. Until this date the airline had flown a total of 8,165,000 miles from its inception in 1937 without a single passenger fatality.

9 December 1956   A TCA North Star crashed into the mountains in British Columbia with the loss of all passengers and crew.

29 November 1963   A DC-8F belonging to TCA crashed on take-off from Montreal with the loss of 118 lives.

5 July 1970   An Air Canada DC-8 crashed near Toronto with the loss of 109 lives.

SOME NOTABLE TCA/AIR CANADA AIRCRAFT

Lockheed 14 Super Electra
U.S. made.

Power plant: 2 1200 h.p. Pratt & Whitney
    Hornet engines.
Wing span: 65'6"
Length: 44'2½"
Height: 11'5½"
Weight loaded: 18,500 lbs.
Cruising speed (sea level): 201 mph
Range with max. payload: 800 statute miles
Passengers: 10 and 3 crew
Cost (new): $130,000.
Lockheed Electra aircraft of all types were in
    TCA service from 1937 to 1949.

Avro Lancastrian
British and Canadian made.

Power plant: 4 Rolls-Royce Merlin engines
Wing span: 102'0"
Length overall: 75'0"
Height: 18'0"
Take-off weight: 63,000 lbs.
Cruising speed: 230 mph
Range: 3,100 statute miles
Max cargo: 9,000 lbs. including mail
Fuel capacity: 3,200 Imperial gallons
Passengers: 10
Cost: Nominal. These aircraft became the
    property of TCA.
First entered TCA service in 1943.

Douglas DC-3 (C47)
U.S. made

Power plant: 2 Pratt & Whitney R1830 en-
   gines
Wing span: 95'0"
Length overall: 64'5"
Max landing weight: 26,000 lbs.
Cruising speed: 160 mph
Max. payload: 5,860 lbs.
Fuel capacity: 670 Imperial gallons
Passengers: 21
Cost: (secondhand) $120,000
First entered TCA service in 1945.

Canadair North Star
Canadian made.

Power plant: 4 Rolls-Royce Merlin 722 &
   724 engines
Wing span: 117'6"
Length overall: 93'10½"
Max. landing weight: 72,000 lbs.
Cruising speed: 220-230 mph
Fuel capacity: 2,350 and 2,908 Imperial gal-
   lons
Passengers: 40 to 62
Cost (new): $700,000
Total number in fleet (all types): 29. These
   aircraft were unpressurized at first, but
   later models were fully pressurized.
First entered TCA service in 1947. All
cargo version retired June 30, 1961.

Bristol Freighter (Wayfarer) Type 170 Mk 31
British made.

Power plant: 2 Bristol Siddeley Hercules 734
    engines
Wing span: 108'0"
Length: 73'4"
Height: 21'8"
Gross weight: 44,000 lbs.
Cruising speed: 165 mph
Cost (average): $328,000
Three of these aircraft first entered TCA service in 1953, and were retired in 1955. These machines were only used for cargo duties.

Lockheed 1049 Super Constellation
U.S. made

Power plant: 4 Wright Compound engines
Wing span: 123'0"
Length overall: 113'7"
Max. landing weight: 113,500 lbs.
Cruising speed: 310 mph
Fuel capacity: 5,452 and 6,466 Imperial gallons
Passengers (all types): 63,71 and 75
Cost (new): $2,300,000
First entered TCA service in 1954, finally retired in January 1962. In all, 14 of these machines served with the airline.

Vickers Viscount
British made

Power plant: 4 Rolls-Royce Dart 506c engines
Wing span: 93'11"
Length overall: 81'2"
Max. landing weight: 54,500 lbs.
Cruising speed: 315 mph
Fuel capacity: 1,950 Imperial gallons
Passengers: 44 before being converted to 54 tourist seats.
Cost (new): $1,000,000
Number in TCA/AC fleet: 51
First entered TCA service in 1955; finally retired from Air Canada in 1974.

Vickers Vanguard
British made

Power plant: 4 Rolls-Royce Tyne R TY-11 engines
Wing span: 118'0"
Length overall: 122'10"
Max. landing weight: 130,500 lbs.
Cruising speed: 415 mph
Fuel capacity: 5,100 Imperial gallons
Passengers: 108
Cost average new (1961): $3,000,000
Number in TCA/AC fleet: 23
First entered TCA service in 1961, retired from passenger service October 1971.

Douglas DC-8
U.S. made

Power plant: 4 Rolls-Royce Conway R.CO 10
    or 12 engines
Wing span: 142'4"
Length overall: 150'9"
Max. landing weight: 202,000/207,000 lbs.
Cruising speed: 550 mph
Range: 4,800 statute miles
Fuel capacity: 18,360 or 19,170 Imperial gal-
    lons
Passengers: 133
Cost (new): $6,000,000
Number in fleet (1977): 35 of all types.
First entered TCA service in 1960.

Douglas DC-9
U.S. made

Power plant: 2 Pratt & Whitney JT8D-7 en-
    gines
Wing span: 93'4"
Length: 119'4"
Height: 27'6"
Max. landing weight: 95,300 lbs.
Cruising speed: 520 mph
Normal cruising altitude: 27,000'-33,000'
Range: 1,780 statute miles
Fuel capacity: 3,550 Imperial gallons
Passengers: 94
Cost (1971): $3,700,000
Number in AC fleet (1977): 50 varied types.
First entered AC service in 1966.

92

Boeing 747
U.S. made

Power plant: 4 Pratt & Whitney JT9D
    engines
Wing span: 196'0"
Length: 231'0"
Height: 63'0"
Max. payload: 130,000 lbs.
Cruising speed: approx 570 mph
Normal cruising altitude: 35,000'
Range: 5,000 statute miles
Fuel capacity: 46,770 Imperial gallons
Passengers: 365
Cost (1971): $23,000,000
    Number in fleet (1977): 6
First entered AC service in 1971.

Lockheed 1011 TriStar
U.S. made

Power plant: 3 Rolls-Royce RB211 engines
Wing span: 155'0"
Length: 178'0"
Height: 55'0"
Max. payload: 83,000 lbs.
Cruising speed: approx. 575-600 mph
Normal cruising altitude: 35,000'
Range: 3,000 statute miles (approx)
Fuel capacity: 20,600 Imperial gallons
Passengers: 256
Cost (1973): $14,000,000 approx.
Number in fleet (1977): 12
First entered AC service in 1973.